Programming in Visual BASIC
for Windows

D1341257

BOOKS AVAILABLE

By both authors:

BP306 A Concise Introduction to Ami Pro 3
BP327 DOS one step at a time
BP337 A Concise User's Guide to Lotus 1-2-3 for Windows
BP341 MS-DOS explained
BP343 A concise introd'n to Microsoft Works for Windows
BP346 Programming in Visual Basic for Windows
BP351 WordPerfect 6 explained
BP352 Excel 5 explained
BP353 WordPerfect 6.0 for Windows explained
BP354 Word 6 for Windows explained
BP362 Access one step at a time
BP372 CA-SuperCalc for Windows explained
BP387 Windows one step at a time
BP388 Why not personalise your PC
BP399 Windows 95 one step at a time*
BP400 Windows 95 explained*
BP402 MS Office one step at a time
BP405 MS Works for Windows 95 explained
BP406 MS Word 95 explained
BP407 Excel 95 explained
BP408 Access 95 one step at a time
BP409 MS Office 95 one step at a time
BP415 Using Netscape on the Internet
BP419 Using Microsoft Explorer on the Internet
BP420 E-mail on the Internet
BP426 MS-Office 97 explained
BP428 MS-Word 97 explained
BP429 MS-Excel 97 explained
BP430 MS-Access 97 one step at a time

By Noel Kantaris:

BP232 A Concise Introduction to MS-DOS
BP258 Learning to Program in C
BP259 A Concise Introduction to UNIX*
BP261 A Concise Introduction to Lotus 1-2-3
BP264 A Concise Advanced User's Guide to MS-DOS
BP274 A Concise Introduction to SuperCalc 5
BP284 Programming in QuickBASIC
BP325 A Concise User's Guide to Windows 3.1

Programming in Visual BASIC for Windows

by

P.R.M. Oliver
and
N. Kantaris

BERNARD BABANI (publishing) LTD.
THE GRAMPIANS
SHEPHERDS BUSH ROAD
LONDON W6 7NF
ENGLAND

PLEASE NOTE

Although every care has been taken with the production of this book to ensure that any projects, designs, modifications and/or programs, etc., contained herewith, operate in a correct and safe manner and also that any components specified are normally available in Great Britain, the Publishers and Author(s) do not accept responsibility in any way for the failure (including fault in design) of any project, design, modification or program to work correctly or to cause damage to any equipment that it may be connected to or used in conjunction with, or in respect of any other damage or injury that may be so caused, nor do the Publishers accept responsibility in any way for the failure to obtain specified components.

Notice is also given that if equipment that is still under warranty is modified in any way or used or connected with home-built equipment then that warranty may be void.

© 1995 BERNARD BABANI (publishing) LTD

First Published – September 1995
Reprinted – October 1996
Reprinted – August 1997
Reprinted – June 1998

British Library Cataloguing in Publication Data:

Oliver, Phil
Programming in Visual Basic for Windows

I. Title II. Kantaris, Noel
005.42

ISBN 0 85934 346 4

Cover Design by Gregor Arthur
Cover Illustration by Adam Willis
Printed and Bound in Great Britain by Cox & Wyman Ltd, Reading

ABOUT THIS BOOK

This book is a guide to programming using Visual BASIC for Windows. The reader is not expected to have any familiarity with the language as both the environment and statements are introduced and explained with the help of simple programs. The user is encouraged to build these, save them, and keep improving them as more complex language statements and commands are encountered.

The book is not intended to replace the very extensive manuals that come with the program, but to complement them. The very size of Visual BASIC and its completely new programming environment, can be very daunting to a new user, so this systematic approach should make learning very much easier.

The first three Chapters give an overview of Visual BASIC and the graphic based environment it uses. Forms and the more simple controls that go with them are introduced, but no attempt is made to explain how to use Microsoft Windows itself. It is assumed that if you want to create programs that work with Windows, you will be familiar with this interface.

Chapters 4-7 cover the programming language and how it is entered into your PC, dealing with the basic Visual BASIC statements which control program flow, input and output, and leading to the concepts of strings and arrays.

In Chapter 8 we return to some of the more powerful controls that allow you to produce the sort of Windows programs that you can buy.

The next chapter covers functions and procedures which expand the programming capabilities of the user beyond the beginner's level. Chapter 10 deals entirely with disc file handling techniques and should be of special interest to those who need to process large quantities of data. The two main types of data files are discussed in some detail, namely, sequential and random access types. The last chapter gives an overview of the powerful debugging features of the program.

Appendices are included that detail all the Event Procedures available in Visual BASIC as well as a brief, but complete, language reference listing.

ABOUT THE AUTHORS

Phil Oliver graduated in Mining Engineering at Camborne School of Mines in 1967 and since then has specialised in most aspects of surface mining technology, with a particular emphasis on computer related techniques. He has worked in Guyana, Canada, several Middle Eastern countries, South Africa and the United Kingdom, on such diverse projects as: the planning and management of bauxite, iron, gold and coal mines; rock excavation contracting in the UK; international mining equipment sales and technical back up and international mine consulting for a major mining house in South Africa. In 1988 he took up a lecturing position at Camborne School of Mines (part of Exeter University) in Surface Mining and Management.

Noel Kantaris graduated in Electrical Engineering at Bristol University and after spending three years in the Electronics Industry in London, took up a Tutorship in Physics at the University of Queensland. Research interests in Ionospheric Physics, led to the degrees of M.E. in Electronics and Ph.D. in Physics. On return to the UK, he took up a Post-Doctoral Research Fellowship in Radio Physics at the University of Leicester, and then in 1973 a lecturing position in Engineering at the Camborne School of Mines, Cornwall, (part of Exeter University), where since 1978 he has also assumed the responsibility for the Computing Department.

TRADEMARKS

ACKNOWLEDGEMENTS

We would like to thank the staff of both Microsoft in the UK and Text 100, for their valuable help and the provision of software for the preparation of this book. We would also like to thank colleagues at the Camborne School of Mines for their helpful suggestions which assisted us in the writing of this book.

PREFACE

Visual Basic is rapidly becoming one of the most popular 'dialects' of BASIC in use today on IBM and compatible computers. It comes in two types, one for the DOS environment, and the other, described in this book, that works with Microsoft Windows.

The original version of BASIC (which stands for Beginner's All-purpose Symbolic Instruction Code) was first developed as a teaching language at Dartmouth College in 1964. In 1978 'standard BASIC' was adopted as a result of recommendations on the minimal requirements of the language.

BASICA, written by Microsoft for use with the IBM PCs, and GWBASIC (its equivalent form running on compatibles), was an enhanced version of standard BASIC, embodying nearly 200 commands. These were bundled with pre-DOS 5 versions of the operating system, but users of MS-DOS 5 and higher have access to a cut-down version of Microsoft's QuickBASIC, known as QBASIC.

QuickBASIC was Microsoft's first *compiled* version of BASIC, the earlier ones being *interpreted* languages. With an interpreted language each and every statement of code has to be interpreted by a separate program called the interpreter before the program is actually run. This happens each time a statement is encountered, even if it appears within a loop. With a compiled language, on the other hand, a separate program, called the compiler, is used to check the whole program for errors and then compiles it into the machine specific code that will actually be executed by the computer at run time. Statements within loops are only checked once, which makes a compiled program far more efficient than an interpreted one.

Visual BASIC is an event driven, or Object Oriented, compiled language that also includes most of the features built into QuickBASIC, so earlier programs can be easily adapted to run on Visual BASIC.

CONTENTS

1. PACKAGE OVERVIEW

Visual BASIC, unlike other structured languages such as C, or QuickBASIC, is an *event driven* programming language. Instead of the program flow being controlled from the written code and running mainly from the first to the last lines of code, it is controlled by interactive events at run-time, such as the clicking of a mouse on a button or form. When such an event occurs, the program code attached to that event is actioned. In the program, buttons, forms, controls, the screen and your printer, etc., are all called *objects* and Visual BASIC is known as an Object Oriented language. It reacts to the manipulation of objects. Once this concept is grasped, the change from other programming languages is much easier.

Versions of Visual BASIC

Visual BASIC is available for working in both the DOS and Windows environments. Although many of the principles are the same with both, this book covers only the versions used under Microsoft Windows. A version of the Windows program (later than v3.0) must be installed and running on your PC before you start.

Since the original Visual BASIC for Windows was released in May 1991 there have been several updates and improvements to the package. At the time of writing, Version 3.0 is the current one. This, like its predecessor, comes in two versions, a standard one for most users; and a Professional Edition with many powerful extras attached to it, and costing several times as much.

As far as this book is concerned, it does not matter which version of Visual BASIC for Windows you have. The examples were all developed with the Professional Edition of Version 3.0, but none of its custom controls were used. In fact they were all disabled so as not to complicate the screen displays more than necessary.

Visual BASIC for Windows provides by far the easiest way for you to produce real working applications (or programs) to run under Windows. Once you have created your application you can very easily produce an executable file (with the extension .EXE) which can then be run without Visual BASIC.

In fact, if it is good enough, you can even distribute your application royalty-free, as long as you have purchased, and registered, your copy of Visual BASIC.

Installing Visual BASIC

The initial installation procedure is very well automated, but before you start, make sure your system is suitable.

System Requirements:

Microsoft specify the following minimum set-up. An IBM compatible PC with an 80286 processor, or higher; with a hard disc, 1MB of memory (RAM), a mouse, an EGA (or better) display, running MS-DOS (version 3.1 or later) and Windows (version 3.0 or later) in standard or enhanced mode.

To make use of the advantages of the Windows interface we would recommend at least a 386 based machine with 4MB of memory and 30MB of spare hard disc space. With anything less, the quality of life can get somewhat strained.

The Installation Process:

To carry out the installation, start Windows in the usual way and insert the Visual BASIC Setup disc (No. 1) in your A: drive. From the Windows Program Manager screen, activate the **File** menu, by clicking your mouse on **File**, then click on **Run** and type

```
A:setup
```

in the **Command Line** box that is opened. Pressing the <Enter> key will produce an opening Welcome Screen with options to **Cancel Setup** or to **Continue**. Click on the **Continue** button, or press the 'C' key (you can action most commands in two ways, either by clicking with the left mouse button, or by pressing the highlighted letter key. Throughout this book the highlighted letter will be shown underlined).

If you are installing from the system discs for the first time, you will be asked for details of your name and company. This information is stored on the first Setup disc and a further installation from the same discs will produce the following fairly strong copyright warning message.

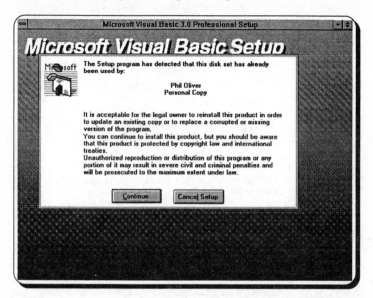

Select **Continue** and you are given the choice of where the program files should be stored. If you are at all in doubt here, choose the default C:\VB, but if you prefer to install it elsewhere, make the required changes. Select **Continue** and if the directory you chose does not exist, you will be given the option to **Create** it.

The next screen, with the Professional Edition, indicates that you need 32MB of available hard disc space. Our set-up only used 26.6MB, but that is still an enormous chunk of most peoples' storage capacity! Select **Complete Installation** if you have enough space, or **Custom Installation** to select what parts of the package to install. Next, we suggest you **Dont install ODBC**, because if you are still reading this section you are almost certainly not going to need database programming links for a while yet.

The file unpacking and copying procedure should then start and the bottom window frame will keep you informed about what is happening. When required, you will be asked to place the next disc into the A: drive.

After about 20 minutes the tedious operation should be complete and you will be given a message to place the command

```
Share.exe /L:500
```

in your AUTOEXEC.BAT command. As far as this book is concerned you can ignore this message, but you may need to remember it at a later stage.

Lastly you should see the Installation Complete box shown above. This gives you the options to **Return to Windows** or to **Run Visual BASIC**. Having spent the last half hour feeding discs into your drive and waiting patiently, we are sure you will want to choose the latter option, but bear with us and return to Windows.

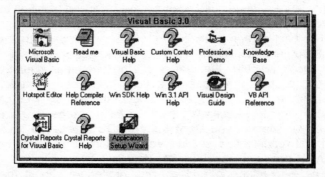

The Professional Edition, as shown above, places 15 icons into a new Visual BASIC group window. Double-clicking the **Read me** icon will open a file of program information that is more recent than the published manuals.

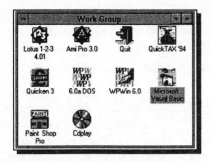

We copied the program start-up icon (the first one in the previous list) into our Work Group window and reduced the other options with their group icon at the bottom of the Program Manager window.

Some Housekeeping

Before getting too involved with Visual BASIC we suggest you carry out the following two housekeeping tasks.

Minimising Program Manager:

As you will soon find out (if you haven't done already), the Visual BASIC working window is most unusual in that it consists, by default, of five different windows superimposed onto whatever screen background was active when the program was opened. This can be most confusing and we recommend that you minimise any other active programs to icons to keep them off the body of the screen.

With the Program Manager itself this is best done with the **Options**, **Minimize on Use** command, as shown here. If you

also check the **Save Settings on Exit** option, open the **File** sub-menu, and select **Exit** while the <Shift> key is depressed, the new setting will be saved without actually having to leave Windows. This is quite a useful and not very well documented trick.

Visual BASIC Directory Structure:

When our version of the program was installed, ten subdirectories were placed on our hard disc, as shown on the next page. At the learning stage, the most useful of these is C:\VB\SAMPLES which contains, as you might expect from its name, a very extensive collection of Visual BASIC sample programs. When you need inspiration it is well worth looking through these for programming ideas.

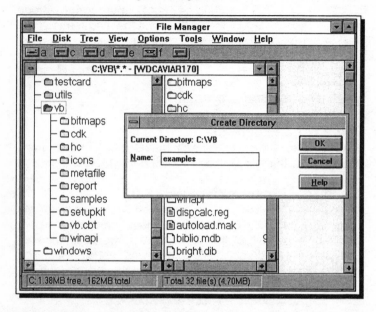

One directory missing from this list is one suitable for storing the programs (called **Projects** in Visual BASIC speak) that you develop yourself. This is easily rectified, with the **File**, **Create Directory** command from the Windows File Manager, as shown above.

Also shown above is the fact that our C: drive was almost wiped out when Visual BASIC was installed. Only 1.38MB of free disc memory is not very clever for the main Microsoft Windows drive. Because of this, we reinstalled Visual BASIC on our E: drive, which explains any drive 'discrepancies' shown in any screen dumps later in the book!

2. THE VISUAL BASIC ENVIRONMENT

Starting the Program from DOS
To start Visual BASIC, as long as the VB directory is included on your system path, you need only type the words **win vb** at the C:\> prompt. Otherwise you must specify the complete path to the directory in the command, maybe as follows:

```
win C:\VB\VB
```

It is more usual however to start the program when Windows is already running as explained below.

Starting the Program from Windows
As we saw in the last chapter, the SETUP program opens a new group window in the Windows Program Manager and places several icons in it.

Microsoft
Visual Basic

Visual BASIC is started in Windows by either double clicking the left mouse button on the program icon shown here, or by double clicking on a Visual BASIC project file (with the extension .MAK) in the Windows' File Manager. In this case the project will be loaded into Visual BASIC at the same time.

General Windows Skills
We have assumed for the remainder of this book that anybody setting out to learn to program in the Windows environment will already be familiar with the workings of the Windows Graphic User Interface (GUI). We do not cover the basics of moving, re-sizing, iconising or generally manipulating windows, of handling the mouse, or menu systems. If you need more information on these skills, we suggest you first work through one of the Concise Guides to Windows listed at the front of this book.

The Visual BASIC Tutorial
Once the program is loaded, maybe the first thing you should do is work through the tutorials which are started with the **Help**, **Learning Microsoft Visual BASIC** menu command.

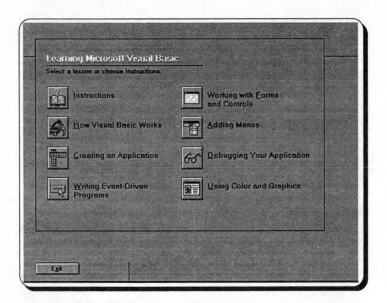

The opening menu above has eight options for you to work through, each taking about 10-15 minutes, and we strongly recommend you do this. A sample screen is shown below.

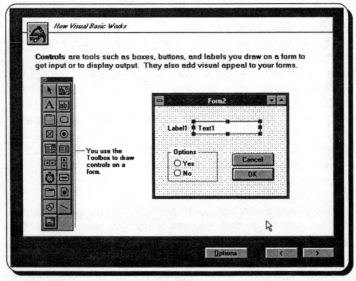

You can of course run through these tutorial exercises as often as you like. When you have finished with a tutorial, either select another from the Main menu screen, or press the E**x**it button.

Programming Steps

With most programming languages you must write countless lines of code into an editor before anything happens. Some of this code might be written to control the operation of the program, but probably most of it will control the screen display and the interface with the final user of the program.

Design Mode:

With Visual BASIC, on the other hand, you do not need to write code to set the program interface; you design this graphically on the screen in 'design mode'. All of the control features you are used to in Windows, such as menu bars, list boxes, control buttons, etc., can be almost instantly placed on 'Forms' at design time. When you are happy with the interface, you then enter code to control how its components interact with each other, and with the final user. Even this operation is made easy in Visual BASIC, which names and controls your input procedures almost automatically.

Break (Debug) Mode:

Many powerful features are built into this mode of Visual BASIC to help you check that your code is correct and to track down problems, as and when they occur.

Run Mode:

When you finally run the program, or project, that you have created, the Forms you designed become the program windows in 'run mode'. This means that Visual BASIC gives you the power to use most of Windows' built-in facilities, like window manipulation, file opening and saving, etc., without having to write much program code at all. You can get really professional output with the minimum amount of effort!

The Visual BASIC Screen

The opening screen of Visual BASIC 3.0 is shown below, with some of the windows slightly rearranged. The Professional Edition also contains 16, more advanced, function icons in the Toolbar on the left, which we will ignore in this book.

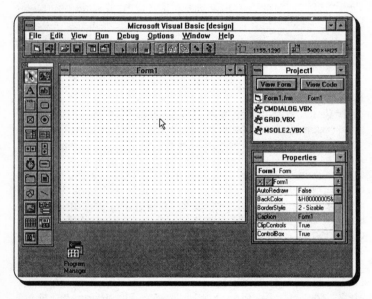

When the program first starts, it is in 'design mode', as shown on the title bar above, with five separate elements making up the screen.

To understand the workings of the program we must spend some time looking at the various parts that make up this screen.

The Help System:

Like most modern Windows based programs, Visual Basic has a very powerful on-line Help facility and when learning the program this is one of the essential tools to use. It is usually easier and quicker to find information this way, than ploughing through the manuals. To demonstrate this, select each of the screen elements, in turn, and press the **F1** key, to

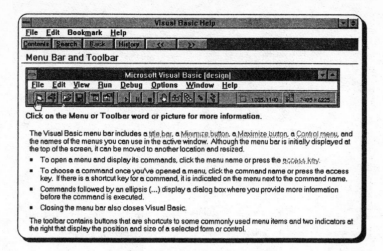

Click on the Menu or Toolbar word or picture for more information.

The Visual Basic menu bar includes a title bar, a Minimize button, a Maximize button, a Control menu, and the names of the menus you can use in the active window. Although the menu bar is initially displayed at the top of the screen, it can be moved to another location and resized.

- To open a menu and display its commands, click the menu name or press the access key.
- To choose a command once you've opened a menu, click the command name or press the access key. If there is a shortcut key for a command, it is indicated on the menu next to the command name.
- Commands followed by an ellipsis (...) display a dialog box where you provide more information before the command is executed.
- Closing the menu bar also closes Visual Basic.

The toolbar contains buttons that are shortcuts to some commonly used menu items and two indicators at the right that display the position and size of a selected form or control.

open its Help screen, then to get details of an individual button, or menu command, click the 'hand' pointer on it.

Title and Toolbar:

As shown above, this screen element contains the main Visual BASIC menu bar, with the normal windows control buttons, as well as the Toolbar. This bar contains 14 buttons, or icons, to give shortcut access to some of the most commonly used menu commands. Some of these are shown below, others will be detailed later as they become relevant to our text. Probably the icons you will use most are the Run and Stop contols.

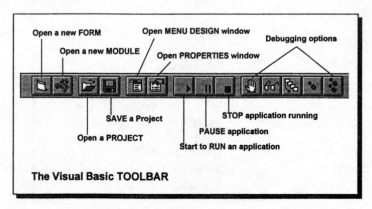

The Visual Basic TOOLBAR

Visual BASIC Forms:

A form is the interface with the application you create. You can have multiple forms and place controls, text boxes and

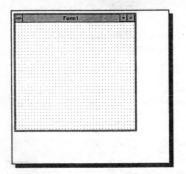

pictures on them when in design mode. What you place on a form is what will be seen in a window when the application is run. To help when placing features on a form, by default, a grid is active, as shown here. When new features are added they automatically align themselves to the nearest grid positions.

The Toolbox:

This is used to place different types of control objects onto a Visual BASIC form.

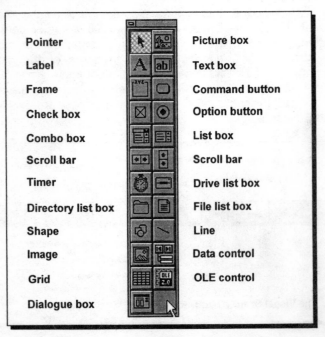

Pointer	Picture box
Label	Text box
Frame	Command button
Check box	Option button
Combo box	List box
Scroll bar	Scroll bar
Timer	Drive list box
Directory list box	File list box
Shape	Line
Image	Data control
Grid	OLE control
Dialogue box	

Project Window:

In Visual BASIC you can only have one project open at a time. The Project window displays a list of all the forms, modules, and custom controls in an open project, or application. From the Project window you can open the Form window for an existing form by selecting its name and clicking the **View Form** button. Similarly, you can open the Code window for an existing form by selecting its name and clicking the **View Code** button.

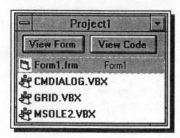

Properties Window:

All the objects you create in Visual BASIC (forms, boxes, command buttons, etc.), have a very detailed set of 'properties' which are controlled from this window. If it is not open, click the Properties icon on the toolbar, or press **F4**.

The **Object Box**, at the top of this window, displays the name of the object whose properties are listed. Clicking its drop-down arrow (on the right) lets you select other objects from a list.

The **Settings Box**, immediately below this, lets you edit the setting of the Property highlighted in the Properties List. Properties often have an existing range of setting options, which can be shown, and selected, by clicking the drop-down arrow to the right of the Settings Box.

The **Properties List** takes up the rest of this window. All the properties available for the selected object are listed, with the current setting shown alongside. You change a property by selecting it in the list, and then either typing a new value in the Settings Box, or making another selection in this box from the drop-down list of those available.

13

A First Program

The next step forward has to be a simple programming example to show how these features fit together.

If Form1 is not open on your screen, select it in the Project1 window and click the View Form button, also in that window. This should also open the Properties window, but if not, press the **F4** key.

Creating an Object:

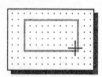

Now, to start, we will add a button to the form. Click the 'Command button' icon in the Toolbox and move the pointer back over the form window. It should change to a cross hair. Position this cross at the place in the form where you want the top left corner of the button, hold down the left mouse button and 'drag' the button shape, as shown here. When you release the mouse button your new button will be placed on the form, with the name 'Command1' placed in it, as shown below.

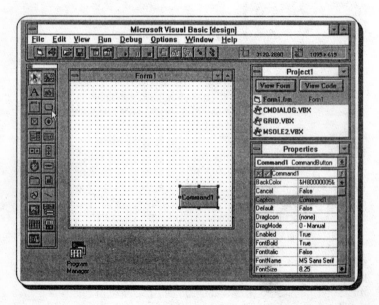

14

During this operation you could have used the two indicators to the right of the Toolbar. The Position Indicator, on the left, shows the position of the top left corner of your button, while the Size Indicator gives its dimensions. By default, these are in 'twips', a standard unit of screen measurement equal to 1/20 of a printers point.

Changing a Caption:
The new button should be 'selected' in the form and have a series of black 'handles' around it. If not, click it with the mouse. Now, look at the Properties window. The highlighted property in the list should be 'Caption', showing as 'Command1'. The caption is what actually appears on the face of the button.

Double click in the Settings box of the Properties window, type **Print** and click the '√' Enter button. The button should now have a new caption on it. Changing an object's properties is as easy as that.

Entering Code:
Now double click on the newly created button. This opens the 'Code window' Form1.frm, with two lines of code and the cursor already placed for you. Type the following text:

```
Print "My first Windows 'program'?"
```

Your window should now look like that below. Don't worry too much about the rest of it at this stage, all will be revealed later.

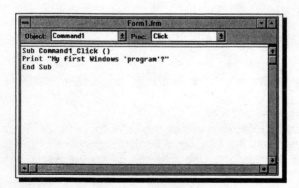

Running a Program:

 For neatness, close the Code window with the <Alt+F4> keys and click the Run Toolbar button (or use **F5**, or the **Run**, **Start** menu command).

Visual BASIC changes to 'Run' mode and displays the window 'Form1' containing our Print button. Clicking the mouse on this button will cause our message to be printed in the window, as shown below.

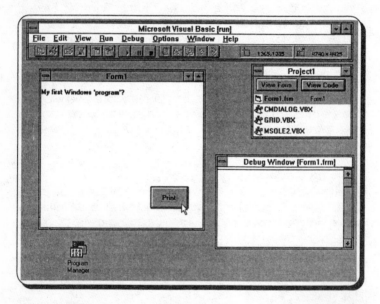

In Run mode all you can do at the moment is print the message every time the button is clicked. Not a very useful program, but it is a start. To stop the program running and return to Design mode click the Stop Toolbar button. The easiest way to move between Run and Design modes is with the Run and Stop Toolbar buttons.

Saving a Program:

We may use this example as the basis for other applications, so save it with the **File**, **Save Project** command, or the Save Project Toolbar icon. Use 'EXAMPLE1' as the name for both the form and project, when asked.

3. PROGRAMMING BASICS

Project Elements

As can be seen from the very simple example of the last chapter, writing a program in Visual BASIC follows a very definite series of steps.

- The interface is designed and built graphically, by placing controls and boxes, etc., on a series of forms.

- The properties of the forms, and controls used, are set to produce the visual results required.

- Code is written to link these up and generally make the program work. Essentially this code

  - controls the general action of the program and,
  - determines how it will react when specific actions are carried out on specific objects by the end user; such as when a button is clicked, or a form double-clicked.

The Interface

This consists of one, or more, forms with control features placed from the Toolbox, to enable the required program functions to be carried out by the final user.

Forms:

A form is a window, that opens at some stage when the program is run, and is used to either show information to, or get it from, the program user. When you start to build a new 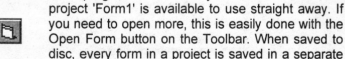 project 'Form1' is available to use straight away. If you need to open more, this is easily done with the Open Form button on the Toolbar. When saved to disc, every form in a project is saved in a separate file with a '.FRM' extension. This makes it possible to use a particular form in several different projects. To include an existing form in an opened project, use the **File**, **Add File** command. It will then be listed, and accessible from, the Project Window. To remove one from an opened project, use the **File**, **Remove File** command.

Controls are the objects that are placed on forms and are described in more detail later.

Modules:
Most of the code in a program, or project, will be included in the various forms of the project. However the code attached to a form is only usable by that form. For code to be available for other forms, or the application as a whole, it must be placed in a separate 'module'.

Code modules are stored with a '.BAS' file extension and are very much like more traditional BASIC programs. They do not have the power to get input from the user, or to create graphic displays.

 To open a module, simply click the Open Module icon, shown here, or use the **File**, **New Module** command from the menu. A module can include:

- **Declarations** of constants, types, variables and DLL procedures.

- **General Procedures** which can be called from anywhere in an application. These can be either **Sub** procedures, that do not return a value, or **Function** procedures, that do return one.

Applications:
An application (or program), is a collection of forms and modules that can be saved together as a project, and can be combined into a single executable file, with an '.EXE' extension. Forms and modules, and their code, can also be incorporated in other applications. As you progress with Visual BASIC you should build up a library of forms and procedures to use time and again. There is no point re-inventing the wheel every time you build a new application!

The AUTOLOAD.MAK File:
This file is included with Visual BASIC and controls the general environment of a newly opened project, as well as which files and custom controls are loaded with it. To change the contents of new projects, use the **File**, **Open Project** and select the file AUTOLOAD.MAK.

18

When the Professional Version of Visual BASIC 3.0 is opened the Toolbox contains 16 more icons than the Standard Version. These are the extra 'custom controls' which have the '.VBX' extension. If not wanted in your new projects these can be removed from this file and, if necessary at a later date, re-loaded with the **File**, **Add File** menu command. We left the three files, GRID.VBX, CMDIALOG.VBX and MSOLE2.VBX, but removed the others, to simplify the screen layouts.

This was done by selecting each file in the Project Window and using the **File**, **Remove File** menu command. If you just delete the files with the File Manager, you will get an error message for each file every time the program starts up, which can become very wearing.

Make any changes to your preferred working environment with the **Options**, **Environment** command and then save the file in the usual way. Every new project that is opened from now on will be controlled by the settings in this AUTOLOAD.MAK file.

Visual BASIC Controls

As mentioned earlier, controls are placed on forms from the Toolbox. The form below shows a composite of the more commonly used controls and which icons are clicked on the Toolbox to produce them.

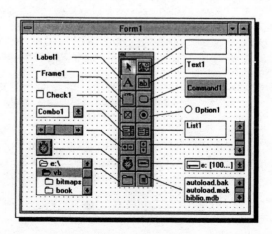

These controls should all be very familiar to any Windows program user. They form the building blocks to make up all types of dialogue boxes.

Picture Box

 Used to display graphical images, or as a container to receive graphical or 'printed' text output.

Label

 Used for text that will not be changed by the user, but can be changed with program code.

Text Box

 Used to hold text that the user can interactively enter or change.

Frame

 Used to create a graphical or functional grouping for controls. To group controls, draw the frame first, then draw controls inside the frame.

Command Button Used to create a button the user can

 click to carry out a command.

Check Box

 Used to create a box that the user can easily choose to indicate if something is true or false, or to display multiple choices when the user can choose more than one.

Option Button

Used in a group of option buttons to display multiple choices from which the user can choose only one.

Combo Box

Used to draw a combination list and text box. The user can either choose an item from the list or enter a value in the text box.

List Box

Used to display a list of items from which the user can choose one. The list can be scrolled if it has more items than can be displayed at one time.

Horiz. Scroll Bar

Used to provide a scrolling tool for quickly moving through a long list of items or information, for showing the current position on a horizontal scale, or as an indicator of speed or quantity.

Vert. Scroll Bar

Used to provide a scrolling tool for quickly moving through a long list of items or information, for showing the current position on a vertical scale, or as an indicator of speed or quantity.

Timer

Used to trap timer events at set intervals. This control is invisible at run time.

Drive List Box

Used to display the valid disc drives in the user's system.

Direct'y List Box

Used to display a hierarchical list of directories on a selected drive.

File List Box

Used to display a file list, that the user can open, save, or otherwise manipulate.

Setting Properties

Once your forms and controls have been chosen and placed, their 'Properties' have to be set in the Properties window, so that they look and behave in the way you want. Most of the default properties will not need to be altered; but some of the more important variables are now described.

Some Form Properties:

When designing a form you can set its position on the screen, and its size, graphically with the mouse. You can also set the *Left, Top, Width* and *Height* properties for more precise control.

The default form settings include a control box, minimise and maximise buttons on the title bar, and a resizeable frame. This lets the final user change the resultant window

with these features, when (s)he runs the program. You can control all of these features though.

Setting the *ControlBox, Min-Button* and *MaxButton* properties to 'False' will turn these features off when the program is run. Changing the settings to 'True' will reactivate them.

The *BorderStyle* property works in conjunction with these in the following ways:

0 - None	Switches off all border or related border elements.
1 - Fixed Single	Can include Control-menu box, title bar, Maximise button, and Minimise button. The window is resizable only using Maximise and Minimise buttons.
2 - Sizable	The default setting. Resizable using any of the optional border elements.
3 - Fixed Double	Can include Control-menu box and title bar; but not Maximise or Minimise buttons. It is not resizable.

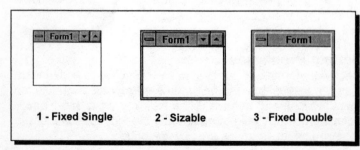

1 - Fixed Single   2 - Sizable   3 - Fixed Double

The best way to get used to all these settings is to change them, one by one, and then click between design and run modes from the Toolbar.

Caption sets what text will display in the title bar, whereas *Name* controls the name of the form itself. Visual BASIC needs every form in an application to have its own distinctive name. They are initially set at Form1, Form2, etc.

BackColor sets the colour of the window, and *ForeColor* the colour of any text which is printed on it at run time. To change the colours simply double-click on the item in the property list and select from the palette which opens. The other attributes of such text can be controlled with the *Text....* properties.

The *Icon* property lets you attach a different icon to your form window, which will show when the window is minimised at run time. You can select from the extensive list of those provided with Visual basic (in the \VB\ICONS directory), or you can design your own.

MousePointer determines the shape of the pointer when it is moved over the window at run time and *Picture* allows you to attach a graphic image 'permanently' to a window. Setting *FontTransparent* to 'True' will then let you print text on the graphic, without blocking it out.

To find out in detail about a particular property, select it in the Properties Window and press **F1**. A full help screen page from the manual is opened.

Label Properties:

A label usually holds text on a form that is not changed interactively by the end user. The *Alignment* property determines whether the *Caption* text is Left, Right or Centre Justified.

When a label has its *AutoSize* property set to 'True', the *WordWrap* setting determines whether it expands vertically or horizontally to fit the text specified in its *Caption* property.

23

With *WordWrap* set to 'True' the text wraps and the label expands, or contracts, vertically to fit the text and the size of the font. The horizontal size does not change.

With the default *WordWrap* setting, 'False', the text does not wrap and the label expands, or contracts, horizontally to fit the length of the text and vertically to fit the size of the font and the number of lines.

To prevent a label changing size at all, leave *AutoSize* with its default setting of 'False'.

Text Box Properties:

A Text Box is used to hold text, entered at design time, interactively by the user, or assigned in code at run time.

The *Text* property contains the text string that is displayed and *MaxLength* determines whether there is a limit to the length of the *Text*. The default is 0, or no maximum. Any number larger than '0' indicates the maximum number of characters that can be entered into the Text Box, (up to a maximum of about 32K).

When *MultiLine* is set to 'True', the *Alignment* property

forces left, right or centre alignment of *Text*; and *ScrollBars* sets scroll bars as follows. The default, 0, sets no bars, 1 sets a Horizontal bar, 2 a Vertical bar and 3 sets both bars, as shown here.

Command Button Properties:

Command buttons are placed on a form so that the end user of the program can select them to begin, interrupt, or end a process. When selected they appear to be depressed.

The *Caption* property determines the text displayed on a command button. Clicking a button always selects it, but there are two other ways that should be used. With the *Default* property set to 'True', pressing <Enter> will select it; and with the *Cancel* property set to 'True' pressing <Esc> will select it. The former would be used to determine what command is actioned in a window when the <Enter> key is pressed, and the latter to control the <Esc> key, maybe for exiting the box, or the program.

Check Box and Option Button Properties:

Check boxes are used to allow the user to easily choose if something is true or false, (switched 'on' or 'off'), or to choose more than one option from a selection. Option Buttons are used in a group to display multiple choices from which the user can select only one. The properties of both are similar. The *Value* property controls what state the object is in. When set at 0, the default, it is unchecked, at 1 it is checked, and at 2 it is greyed out, or dimmed.

When the *Enabled* property is set to 'True', the control is able to respond to events, such as a click from the mouse pointer. When set at 'False' it is inactive.

A frame would usually be used for grouping option button, or check box controls.

The Tab Order of Controls:

When a Windows dialogue box is active only one control on it has the 'focus' at any one time. This is shown by either a dotted box, or a highlight, on the control. You move the focus round the box with the <Tab> key. When the <Tab> key is used in this way the current control 'receives the focus'. When you design a form you should make sure the tab order of the controls on the form is correct.

Initially the order is set automatically and is the same as the order in which you placed the controls. This order is actually controlled by the *TabIndex* properties of the various controls on a form. The control which will receive the focus when a window is opened should have a *TabIndex* value of '0', followed by values of 1, 2, etc.

To prevent the focus being given to a control you can set its *TabStop* property to 'False'. Although the control still holds its place in the tab order, determined by the *TabIndex* property, the focus will not be given to it.

Shortcut Keys:

There is yet another way to select some of the controls in a running window; by pressing an <Alt+letter key> combination from the keyboard. To do this you place an ampersand, the '&' character, in front of the selected letter in the *Caption* property. This underlines the next letter on the control face.

Most of the properties described so far are set during the initial design process. Many of them, however, will also be changed while the program is being run. This is done, either interactively by the user, or under the control of code written into the program.

Writing Code

Visual BASIC is unlike any other programming language we know. Most of the hard work building interfaces, etc., is done almost automatically for you, once you know how to steer the process. Lines of code are required, however, to string all the building blocks together and actually produce useful results.

It is very much an **event-driven procedure** based language, with each independent procedure designed to carry out a specific task. An event being an action which is recognised by a form or control.

Code Windows:

The operation of writing your code is carried out in a special editor called a Code Window. There are two main ways of opening a Code window in design mode. The easiest is to double-click on the form, or control, whose code you want to edit. You can also select the form or control (in other words make it active by clicking it), and press the View Code button in the Project window.

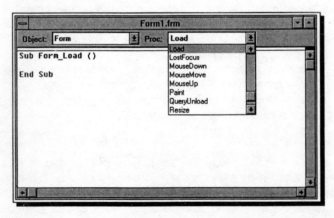

A Code window contains two drop-down list boxes in its top bar. The **Object** box lists the current form and all the controls on it, when you click its down button. The other, with the title **Proc:**, is the **Procedure** box, which lists all the events recognised by Visual BASIC for the form or control displayed in the Object box.

Every form and control has a set of predefined events that it can recognise. The example on the previous page shows the events list opened for the empty form 'Form1'. The active event in the list is 'Load' and the code in the form for that event is shown, ready to edit, in the lower half of the window. When you select an event, either the event procedure associated with that event name, or a code template for the event, is displayed in the bottom part of the Code window.

Any code placed in this Load Procedure would be activated when the form was first opened. In this case, as the form is Form1 and would open first, the code would activate when the program is first run.

You write code to attach event procedures only for events to which you want a form or control to respond. If you leave an event procedure empty that event will produce no program action.

When writing code to attach an event procedure to a form or control you do the following:

1   Select the event in the Procedure box for which you want to add code.
2   Enter your code, in the template provided, in the standard way for entering code and declarations.
3   If necessary, select other forms or controls from the Object box in the Code window and follow the same process from step 1 above.
4   When finished, close the Code window by double-clicking its control box.

Instead of using the template provided by Visual BASIC, you can also create a new procedure by typing

```
Sub ProcedureName
```

in the Code window. In the future, you can find this procedure by selecting (general) from the Object box and then looking in the Procedure box.

Visual BASIC Naming Convention

The standard syntax when writing an event procedure is made easier for you, as Visual BASIC provides the names for procedures automatically. It combines the control name with the event name and separates them with an underscore character '_'. Thus the standard name is

```
Control_Event
```

In the open Code window shown several pages back, the procedure name shown was

```
Form_Load
```

This names the procedure that will activate whenever that form is loaded, or opened. This convention might seem a little confusing to start with, but it is so logical it soon becomes second nature.

The full syntax for an event procedure is:

```
Sub ControlName_EventName (arguments)

    Local variable and constant definitions
    Statements

End Sub
```

Naming Control Properties:

The control properties, described earlier in the chapter, are frequently assigned values or have their values changed, in program code. The usual format for this would be

```
ControlName.Property = expression
```

Where **ControlName** is the name of the control, **Property** is the Visual BASIC name of the property concerned and **expression** is a valid expression (such as a text string, or arithmetic calculation). Note the '.' separating the property name. As an example, the code

```
Text1.Text = "Type a number here"
```

would place the text string 'Type a number here' into the *Text* property of the Text Box named 'Text1'. When this code is activated, that is the message that will show in that Text box on the form.

4. STARTING TO PROGRAM

BASIC Statements

With what was discussed previously in mind, activate Visual BASIC and make sure the 'Syntax Checking' option is set to 'Yes' in the Environment Options box opened with the **Options**, **Environment** command. This ensures that every entered line of code is checked for errors, with minor errors being corrected automatically. We will now create a program to calculate the average of three numbers, in order to demonstrate a few points.

Unlike QuickBasic, you can't just type code into the program and show the printed results straight to the screen when you run the code. The **Print** command does not print to the screen, but will print (after a fashion) to the background of a window. However, if there are any controls on the window, in the print area, they will block out the print output. A picture box receives print output better, but for the moment we will stick to using a window.

Using the **File**, **Open Project** command, open the program EXAMPLE1, which should have been saved from Chapter 2. If not, take a few minutes and do the very basic example now. We will adapt Form1 as a work area for developing some programs to help come to terms with the basics of the programming language.

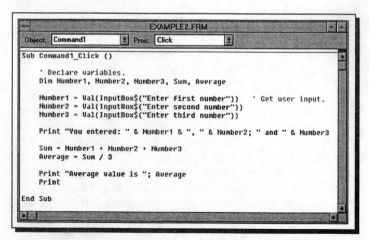

Editing Code:

Double-click on the Print command button which should open the Code Window with the Command1_Click procedure. Delete the middle line of code, by selecting it and pressing the <Del> key, and type in the code shown on the previous page. This is presented to give you an idea of a Visual BASIC source program. The statements in it will be discussed in more detail in the following pages, so there is no need to worry! But you will get some experience of the editor.

When you have entered a row of code, press the <Enter> key to start a new one. Note how the editor changes the entered code. It places spaces in the line, capitalises keywords, checks the line for syntax errors and changes the colour of much of the code. By default, Keywords are coloured red and Comment text is coloured green in the Code window. You can customise these colours in the Environment Options box. We have also set Identifier text to show in violet in our version. These colours make reading the code very much easier.

If you attempt to leave a code line which contains an error, a message box, maybe similar to the one shown here, will open. Pressing the <Esc> key, or clicking the **OK** button, will remove the box. You can then correct the code straight away, or in the future. These messages can be a nuisance if you use the **Cut** and **Paste** facilities of the **Edit** menu. If so, you could turn off the 'Syntax Checking' option, but we wouldn't recommend this.

Before running your code, return to the design form, select the Print command button, press the <Ctrl+C> Copy keys, followed by Paste, <Ctrl+V>. You could also use the **Edit** menu commands, but using the menu is nowhere near as fast. Answer **No** to the question about creating a control array, (we don't want to know about such things at this stage!) and drag the newly placed button until it is placed below the other. Now change its *Caption* property to 'Quit'. At this stage, that should be no problem, otherwise read through the last two chapters again!

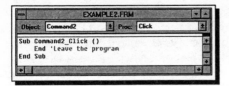

It is always a good idea to give the user of a program an easy way to leave it. Open the Code window for the Quit button and place the very lengthy code statement, shown above, in the Click procedure. The **End** keyword stops any more code being looked at by Visual BASIC and hence ends the program.

Now to test the program out, click the Run Toolbar icon and your new window, with its two buttons, should open. Clicking the Quit button, should place you straight back to design mode. If not, check that the one word of code was entered properly!

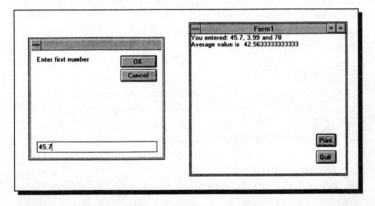

Clicking the Print button, should open an Input Box, as shown on the left in the above composite, in which you enter data manually, in our case a number. Typing in a number and clicking the **OK** button will save the number as variable 'Number1' and open the Box again for 'Number2'.

When all three numbers are entered, the first Print command is actioned, the Sum and Average variables are calculated, and the final result is printed on the form, followed by a blank line (as shown on the right above).

All of which took many times longer to read, than to actually do!

Program Comments:

Our procedure code consists of statements and Comment, or remark lines. Program Comments follow an apostrophe character ('), which can be placed anywhere on a line. Any text that follows this has no effect on the running of a program. This allows the insertion of remarks in the code to help the user remember the function of program sections.

Variables and Constants

Variables:

A variable is a quantity, or a string of text, that is referred to by name, such as Number1, Number2, Number3, Sum and Average in the previous program. Variables can take on many values during program execution, but you must make sure that they are given an initial value, as Visual BASIC automatically zeros numerical variables, and 'empties' text ones, when a program starts.

Constants:

A constant is a quantity that either appears as a number (3 in the seventh executable statement in the previous program) or is referred to by name, but has only one value during program execution, allocated to it by the user.

Expressions:

An expression, when referred to in this text, implies a constant, a variable or a combination of either or both, separated by arithmetic operators.

Naming Convention:

Variable and constant names are formed by combining upper and lower case letters with numbers and the underscore character (_). Other characters and spaces are not valid and the first character must be a letter. The length of the name must not exceed 40 characters. When naming your variables, you must be careful not to use a name which is the same as a Visual BASIC reserved word, otherwise you will get an error message.

To maintain compatibility with earlier versions of BASIC you can add the following suffix characters (%, &, !, #, @, and $) to constants to identify their type. A%, for example, would always be treated as an Integer by Visual BASIC.

The very powerful *Variant* data type is the default for Visual BASIC. This is the data type that is allocated to your variables if they are not explicitly declared as some other type. The Variant data type has no type-declaration character (suffix) and is a special data type that can contain numeric, string, date, or currency data as well as the special values Empty and Null.

There are a variety of other, more conventional, data types for both variables and constants; the most commonly used being the *Integer* and *Single* (single-precision floating-point) types. An integer type can hold only integer (or whole number) quantities and is distinguished from a floating-point type which holds numbers containing fractional parts. The computer stores these two types differently and tends to calculate much faster when using integer-value variables or constants.

Examples of integer and floating-point numbers are as follows:

-255	is an integer number
26.75	is a real, or floating point number
-.45E+16	is an exponential number. The E stands for 'times ten to the power of'.

Less commonly used types of numerical variables and constants are *Long* (long integers) and *Double* (double-precision floating- point). In Visual BASIC, the values of single-precision variables are accurate to 6 significant figures, while those of double-precision variables are accurate to 16. *String* variables can be as long as 65,500 characters.

As we saw above, you do not need to set the type of a variable, as by default, it will be a Variant and adapt to the data involved. There are many times, however, when you will find it necessary to force a specific data type in your code.

The following table shows the fundamental data types supported by Visual BASIC, with their type-declaration suffix and the possible range of each data type.

Type	Suffix	Range
Variant	None	Any numeric value up to the range of a Double or any character text.
Integer	%	-32,768 to 32,767
Long	&	-2,147,483,648 to 2,147,483,647
Single	!	-3.402823E38 to -1.401298E-45 for -ve values; 1.401298E-45 to 3.402823E38 for +ve values
Double	#	1.79769313486232E308 to -4.94065645841247E-324 for -ve values; 4.94065645841247E-324 to 1.79769313486232E308 for +ve values
Currency	@	-922,337,203,685,477.5808 to 922,337,203,685,477.5807
String	$	0 to approximately 65,500 bytes

String Variables:
A sequence of characters is referred to as a literal, and a literal in quotation marks is called a string. For example, ABC123 is a literal, and "ABC123" is a string.

Like numbers, strings can be assigned to variables. They can be distinguished from numeric variables by a $ after the name, for example A$. A string can be assigned to a string variable with a statement such as

```
A$ = "ABC123"
```

Variable Type Declarations:
As with QuickBASIC, variable types can be declared with the use of the **Deftype** statement rather than using type declaration characters. This method however is really kept only to maintain compatibility. Using Dim type declaration statements is far easier.

34

The various Deftype declaration statements are as follows:

Deftype	*Type of Variable*
DefVar letter1 [-letter2]	Variant
DefInt letter1 [-letter2]	Integer
DefLng letter1 [-letter2]	Long
DefSng letter1 [-letter2]	Single
DefDbl letter1 [-letter2]	Double
DefCur letter1 [-letter2]	Currency
DefStr letter1 [-letter2]	String.

Named variables cannot be defined with the Def statement; what can be defined are all variables *starting* with the letter specified within the Def statement (as letter1 above). Ranges of variables can be entered with a hyphen in between their respective starting letters.

For example, to define all variables starting with letters within the range from I to N as integers, you could use

```
DefInt I-N
```

If a floating-point operand is assigned to an integer operand, the floating-point number is first rounded and then truncated to an integer, i.e., assuming that both I and K have been declared as integers (either by the statement **Defint** I-K, or with **Dim..As**), the statements I=3.5 and K=0.37 will cause Visual BASIC to assign the integer values of 4 and 0 to the constants I and K, respectively. For this precise reason, mixing floating-point constants or variables with integers in arithmetic operations, can have unexpected results! Thus, mixed mode arithmetic is best avoided.

The Dim Statement:

In Visual BASIC this is the standard way to declare variables and allocate storage space to them. It was not strictly necessary in our program here (EXAMPLE2), but was used because it is considered good programming practice to declare and dimension any variables you use.

Dim on its own, as used in EXAMPLE2, simply declares what variables are used. They will be treated by the program as the Variant type.

To implicitly declare a variable's type the format is

```
Dim Variable_Name As Type
```

Where **Type** is one of those in the earlier list. Thus the statement

```
Dim I As Integer
```

declares the variable 'I' and ensures that it will always be considered as an integer. Remember that with Visual BASIC, each variable must be declared with its own **As** statement.

It is usual to place Dim statements before any other code. When used in the Declarations section of a form or module, the variables declared with Dim are available to all procedures within the form or module. When used at the procedure level, as in our example, the variables are available only in that procedure.

The Val Function:

This returns the numeric value of a string of characters. In our case, in EXAMPLE2, we did not prevent non numeric values being entered at run time. The Val function stops reading the string at the first character that it cannot recognise as part of a number. Val also strips blanks, tabs, and line feeds from an argument string.

The InputBox$ Function:

This function displays a prompt in a dialogue box, waits for the user to input text or choose a button, and returns the string contents of the text box. The syntax for the function is

```
InputBox[$](prompt [,[title]])
```

where:

prompt   is the string expression displayed as the message in the box.

title   is the optional string expression displayed in the title bar of the dialogue box. If you omit the title, nothing is placed in the title bar.

If you click the **OK** button or press <Enter>, the **InputBox$** function returns whatever is in the text box. Clicking the Cancel button returns a null string ("").

We could also, in our example, have used an **InputBox** function (without the $). This returns a variant type variable, instead of a string.

The **InputBox$** statements provide one way of giving the variables in our example a value. The values for the variables Number1, Number2 and Number3 are entered directly from the keyboard. Once variables have values, they can be used in assignment statements and/or expressions in the rest of the program to perform desired calculations. A variable must have a value before it is used in an expression or in the right hand side of an assignment statement.

The Print Statements:

The **Print** statements allow the printing of the result of our calculation. This result is held in the variable named Average. A string within full quotes following the **Print** command allows us to explain what is printed out. The statement **Print**, with no destination given, causes output to be sent to the current window. Note the use of the ampersand character '&' to concatenate strings and variables in one of the print statements. The statement **Print** on its own on a line, causes the program to print an empty line. This is useful for splitting up print output.

We will delay discussion on formatting output until the next chapter. However, the penalty of this in our program, is that we have to accept the default Visual BASIC form of printing without any control on the number of digits printed out.

Arithmetic Operators & Priority

We shall now examine how the various arithmetic operations in this program are performed. The calculations in the program are performed by the statements

```
Sum = Number1 + Number2 + Number3
Average = Sum/3
```

Combining them into one line, we could also write

```
Average = (Number1 + Number2 + Number3)/3
```

but **Not**

```
Average = Number1 + Number2 + Number3/3
```

It is important that the numerator of this expression is in brackets. If it were not, BASIC would evaluate first Number3/3 and then add to it Number1+Number2, which would give the wrong result. This is due to an inbuilt system of priorities as shown in the table below:

Arithmetic Operators and their Priority

Symbol	Example	Priority	Function
( )	(A+B)/N	1	Parenthesised operation
^	A^N	2	Raise A to the Nth power
*	A*N	3	Multiplication
/	A/N	3	Division
+	A+N	4	Addition
–	A–N	4	Subtraction

Additional Operators:

There are two operators which are useful when performing integer division. These are \ and **Mod**. The \ operator gives the whole number part of the result of a division, while the **Mod** operator gives the remainder (test these in a window). For example, the program statement

```
Print 10\3
```

gives the result 3, while the program statement

```
Print 10 Mod 3
```

gives the result 1.

It must be stressed, however, that the numbers on which integer division (\) and **Mod** operate (called the operands) are first rounded up or down and then converted to integers. Thus, the statements

```
Print 10.1\3.1
Print 10.1 Mod 3.1
```

will give the same result as before, namely 3 and 1, while

```
Print 10.9\3.9
```

`Print 10.9 Mod 3.9`

will give the result of 2 and 3, respectively.

Visual BASIC evaluates expressions, in the order of priority indicated in the table above. Expressions in parentheses are evaluated first; nested groups in parentheses are evaluated beginning with the innermost grouping and working outwards.

Through the use of parentheses, the order of priority of execution, and therefore the final value of an expression, can be changed. If a line has an expression which contains several operators of equal priority, Visual BASIC will evaluate them from left to right.

Let us examine how a complicated expression such as

$$Y = (A+B*X)^2/C-D*X^3$$

is evaluated. We assume that A, B, C, D and X have values.

First the parenthesised portion of the expression will be evaluated. Within these parentheses the multiplication has a higher priority and therefore it will be evaluated first. Then, A will be added to it, resulting in a numerical value to which we will assign the letter Z. Now the expression is reduced to the following:

$$Y = Z^2/C-D*X^3$$

The above has two exponential expressions, the leftmost of which is evaluated first. Writing Z_1 for the result of Z^2 and X_1 for the result of X^3, the expression is now reduced to

$$Y = Z_1/C-D*X_1$$

Again, since division and multiplication have the same priority, the leftmost expression is evaluated first. Finally, the result of the multiplication is taken away from the result of the division and assigned to Y.

All this procedure is carried out automatically by Visual BASIC, but if you intend to use complicated mathematical expressions you must be familiar with it.

The Assignment Statement:
Note that what appears as an equation above is, in fact, an assignment statement and not an algebraic identity. As long as the values of variables on the right of an equals sign are

known, the calculated result will be assigned to the variable on the left of the equals sign.

As an example, consider the following lines:

```
K = 0
K = K + 1
Print K
```

where the second line would be meaningless had it been an algebraic expression. In computing terms the statement means 'take the present value in K, add one to it and store the result in K'. When this line is executed, the value of K (set in the first line) is zero and adding one to it results in a new value of K equal to one. On running this program, Visual BASIC will print the result

```
1
```

in the current window.

Saving a Program

You can save a program by selecting the **F**ile, **Sa**ve **Project** option which will save the current project (.MAK) and all forms and modules in it. If you have any new forms or modules, you'll be prompted to save them, one at a time. The filename you type in, must not be longer that 8 alphanumeric characters (letters and numbers). Visual BASIC automatically adds the default file-name extension .MAK for projects, .FRM for forms, and .BAS for modules.

In our case, save the program as EXAMPLE2.MAK, so that you can modify it in the future, **BUT** make sure you save the form as EXAMPLE2.FRM. If you don't rename your forms for each example, you will end up overwriting the previous 'FORM1' every time.

If you wish to rename an already named program, then use the **F**ile, **Sav**e **Project As** command, which displays a dialogue box, asking you for the new name of the project. Simply type a new name, which will replace that shown in the **File Name** box. Remember to change the **Dri**v**es** and **Directories** settings, if different from the default before pressing <Enter>, or the **OK** button.

Saving Files:

When you want to save the active form, or module, to disc you use the **File**, **Save File**, or **Save File As**, commands in the same way. You might want to do this so that a form or module is available, under a new name, for a different project.

Forms and modules can be stored in text format or in binary (machine code) format. If you select **Save As Text** in the dialogue box the current file will be saved in text format, otherwise files are saved in binary format. Binary format runs much more quickly, but text format programs include all the property settings and can be read with a text editor. This gives you the ability to print on paper all the code controlling the design of your forms and controls, and is a useful way of transporting code, say from a magazine article or book. Our Appendix A contains the code of one of our example programs saved in this way.

Depending on the complexity of the program, you could either rebuild it by matching all the settings manually, or if you are happy typing lots of material, enter the code as it stands into a text editor.

The **File**, **Save Text** command, on the other hand, simply saves the code contained on a form or module. It lists all the contained procedures one by one, but saves no property details. This method is used later in the book to show the contents of some of the example programs.

Importing a Text File:

You can import a text file containing code into a Visual BASIC project and use it with your own code. To do this, choose **Load Text** from the **File** menu, select the file you want to import. Then choose:

Replace to replace all the existing code in the current code window with the imported text.

Merge to add the imported text at the insertion point.

New to load the text into a new module.

5. INPUT AND OUTPUT CONTROL

A program can be made to assign values to variables by either entering information on the keyboard, reading information included with the code, or reading information from data files. Output can be directed to a picture box or window, sent to the printer, or written into a file. Reading input from a data file and writing output to a data file will be dealt with in a separate section.

Text Box Input:
Text boxes can be used on a form to enter data from the keyboard. We have already used the InputBox statement earlier on, but we will examine the other method now. This will be illustrated by writing a program to calculate and display 15% of any number input into a text box.

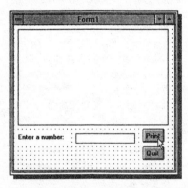

Open the previous program, EXAMPLE2.MAK and add a Picture Box, Label and Text Box, as shown here. We will use the Picture Box as a print area, the Text Box as an input area (so that the user can get information to the code), the Print button to start the calculation and print output process and the Quit button to close.

Change the *Caption* property of Label1 to "Enter a number:" and delete the *Text* property in Text1's property list, by selecting it and pressing the <Del> or <Delete> key, to ensure that the box is empty when the program starts. While still in this list, set the *TabIndex* property to '0', to ensure that the focus is also in this empty box at start up.

As the Print button will control what action this program carries out we must write suitable code in its 'Click' procedure. Double-click the Print button, to open its Code window, delete the previous code between the Sub and End Sub statements and type in the following.

```
Sub Command1_Click ()      ' PerCent program
    Dim Percent As Integer        ' Dimension variables
    Dim Number As Single
    Dim Value As Single

    Percent  = 15
    Number = Val(Text1.Text)           ' Get number
    Value = Number * Percent / 100

    Picture1.Print Percent; "% of"; Number;
    Picture1.Print "="; Value

    Text1.Text  = ""             ' Empty the TextBox
    Text1.SetFocus               ' Place focus in TextBox
End Sub
```

In the above, the keywords that are shown red on the screen are highlighted, and comment text (green on screen) is in

italics. You do not need to worry too much about spaces inside the statements, as the editor will sort this out for you. Leaving empty lines in the code does not affect the running of a program, but can make the code easier to read.

Save the program and form as EXAMPLE3, and then try running it. Every time you enter a number and press the Print button, a result line is printed in the Picture Box.

The code above declares three variables to be used in the routine, one as Integer type and the others as Single. If necessary, look back at the last chapter to see the difference. The 'Percent' variable is set as a constant with the statement

```
Percent  = 15
```

This is one way of giving a value to a variable, but the value cannot be changed, except by another similar statement in the code.

44

The next line

```
Number = Val(Text1.Text)
```

is much more flexible. The value placed in the variable 'Number' depends on the text in Text Box 'Text1' at the time the Print button was pressed.

The **Val** function is there to ensure that only numeric data is passed to the variable. If you try entering different combinations of numbers and letters, you will see very quickly how **Val** works. It accepts any numeric entry until a non-number character is entered and ignores anything else. If you enter '556PP89007', for example, only the number 556 will be passed.

Changing a Property:

The last two lines of code in EXAMPLE3.MAK change two of the properties of the Text Box, named Text1, when that section of the code is run.

At any one time the *Text* property of a Text Box determines what will be displayed in that box. In our program, once a number is entered, processed and printed, we do not want it to still display in the input box as it would interfere with future entries. The statement

```
Text1.Text  = ""
```

resets the *Text* property to contain whatever is held between the inverted commas. In other words, nothing. Note that ("") is, in Visual BASIC, a string **not** a zero. If, as in our case, you want to use the box contents for numerical calculations, a 'Mixed Variables' error will be developed, unless you convert the string to a number with the **Val** function.

Setting an Object's Focus:

The user of our program can only enter numbers into Text1 when the Text Box 'has the focus'. The box is then active with the insertion point placed in it. Earlier on we set the *TabIndex* property to '0', to ensure that the focus is in the box at start up. This can also be done in code, as with the line

```
Text1.SetFocus
```

which places the focus in the empty Text Box, ready to receive new input from the keyboard.

More on Print Output

In the last program, the lines of code

```
Picture1.Print Percent; "% of"; Number;
Picture1.Print "="; Value
```

control what is printed by our program and where it is placed. Picture1.**Print** will send print output to the Picture Box named Picture1 and start printing at the beginning of its top line.

Print, on its own, will send output to the current form itself,

(the one holding the code), as shown here. This also shows that the print result flows behind any controls on the window; the Picture Box frame, in our example. Printed output to a form, or Picture Box, does not scroll when it reaches the end of the print area. Any further output is simply lost.

If variables within a Print statement are separated by semicolons, Visual BASIC writes their value close together with no intervening space. If you leave spaces, when entering code, they will be replaced with semicolons when you move out of the line. A semicolon at the end of a line, as above, will force the next Print statement to continue on that line.

If variables within a Print statement are separated by commas the values of these variables are displayed on the same line, left-justified within inbuilt print zones. These print zones have a width of 14 'average' characters of the font and size that is being used. As most fonts these days are proportional (the widths of characters displayed vary with their size) such output can be erratic, especially if you want neatly lined up columns!

If a string is included within a Print statement, such as "% of" in our example, on execution Visual BASIC displays the actual characters within the quotation marks exactly as they appear in the statement. It is a way of providing captions or headings for the output.

Formatting with Tabs:

Presentation of tabular results can often be made easier to understand by using custom Tabs with the Print statement which allows output to be displayed in columns of your own design.

The program below illustrates the use of this feature.

```
Sub Form_Click ()    ' Use of Print Tabs

    A = 15: B = 25: C = 10: D = 20

    Print Tab(5); "A"; Tab(10); "B"; Tab(15); "C"; Tab(20); "D"
    Print Tab(4); A; Tab(9); B; Tab(14); C; Tab(19); D

End Sub
```

To enter it as EXAMPLE4.MAK, type the code as a Click procedure in the Form Code Window of a new file. When you run the program, click the window that opens, to activate the code. This simple method is useful for testing the code we present, as well as the numerous examples given in the Help section of Visual BASIC. If you like, you can maximise the window to 'simulate' the older type Basic program environment.

On Running this program, Visual BASIC will respond by writing the following to the window

```
A     B     C     D
15    25    10    20
```

Another useful formatting function is the **Print Spc** statement which provides a number of spaces between the last printed position and the next one. For example, the first Print line of the previous program could be replaced by

```
Print Spc(4); "A"; Spc(4); "B"; Spc(4); "C"; Spc(4); "D"
```

which would give a similar output if you were using a non proportional font, such as Courier New. To try this place the following two lines before the above Print statements. As you can see, it is quite easy to control the font style of the printed output.

```
Form1.FontName = "Courier New"
Form1.FontSize = 10
```

The **Print Tab** or **Print Spc** statements cannot be used to move to the left of a current printing position in a given line. Only progressive moves to the right are obeyed.

Note: Although tabulation using the **Tab** and **Spc** statements can work very well with whole numbers, using this method to format tables with floating-point numbers doesn't always work because of the number of significant digits.

Print Locations:

The Visual BASIC co-ordinate properties *CurrentX* and *CurrentY* positions the 'print head' at any point on the object (e.g. Form or Picture Box), and printing starts on that location, irrespective of the print head's previous position.

CurrentX determine the horizontal and *CurrentY* the vertical co-ordinates for the next printing operation.

Co-ordinates are measured from the upper-left corner of a Form or Picture Box object, with *CurrentX* being 0 at an object's left edge and *CurrentY* 0 at its top edge. By default, co-ordinates are expressed in *twips*, or the current scale defined by the *ScaleHeight*, *ScaleWidth*, *ScaleLeft*, *ScaleTop*, and *ScaleMode* properties of the object being printed on.

The **Cls** (Clear Screen) command clears the current print object, (Form or Picture Box), and sends the print head to the upper left-hand corner of the screen, position (0,0). You could place the command code

```
Picture1.Cls
```

in the Code Window of a command button. In which case clicking the button would clear the Picture Box Picture1, ready for new print output.

The next programs give examples of the co-ordinate system usage, the first prints an asterisk character (*) in the middle of a window opened to full screen. Type the code as a Click procedure in the Form Code window of a new file and change the following Form properties.

Property	*Setting*
ScaleMode	4 - Character
WindowState	2 - Maximized

ScaleMode determines the dimension units used in window settings and the above sets the dimensions as characters. With a maximised *WindowState* and the font style used, of 10 Point, Courier New, a window on our screen was 80 characters wide and 29 characters high. With a higher resolution screen setting, yours might not be quite the same.

```
Sub Form_Click ()                    ' Program EXAMPLE5.MAK'
    Form1.FontName = " Courier New"  ' Set font style
    Form1.FontSize = 10

    Form1.CurrentX = 39 ' Position at window centre
    Form1.CurrentY = 14
    Form1.Print "*"        ' Print asterisk
End Sub
```

The *CurrentX* and *CurrentY* properties in the following program place an asterisk at each corner of an 80 character wide x 29 high screen. Note that position (0,0) is the top left corner position, not (1,1), as we would have expected. So position 79 in used the X-direction, instead of position 80 when placing the asterisks at the right edge of the screen.

```
Sub Form_Click ()                ' Program EXAMPLE6.MAK
    Form1.FontName = "Courier New"       ' Set font
    Form1.FontSize = 10

    Form1.CurrentX = 0    ' Position top left
    Form1.CurrentY = 0
    Form1.Print "*"

    Form1.CurrentX = 79   ' Position top right
    Form1.CurrentY = 0
    Form1.Print "*"

    Form1.CurrentX = 0    ' Position bottom left
    Form1.CurrentY = 28
    Form1.Print "*"

    Form1.CurrentX = 79   ' Position bottom right
    Form1.CurrentY = 28
    Form1.Print "*"

End Sub
```

This program has repeated statements and would obviously benefit from some of the techniques covered in the next Chapter.

Formatting Functions

Up to now we have let Visual BASIC display numbers with no regular structure, but just 'how they come'. This is sometimes satisfactory, but when not, the program has a very powerful formatting facility, the **Format$** function. This converts any number to a string with a specific number, date or time format according to the instructions contained in a 'format expression', (shown as "format name" below).

```
Format$(variable, "format name")
```

The easy way to format numbers is to use the following set of common formats that have been built into Visual BASIC.

Format name	*Description*
General Number	Displays the number as it is, with no thousand separators.
Currency	Displays the number with thousand separators and two digits to the right of the decimal point. Displays negative numbers in parentheses.
Fixed	Displays at least one digit to the left and two digits to the right of the decimal separator.
Standard	Displays numbers with thousand separators and two digits to the right of the decimal separator.
Percent	Displays numbers, multiplied by 100, with two digits to the right of the decimal separator and followed by a percent sign (%).
Scientific	Uses standard scientific notation.
Yes/No	Displays **No** if number is 0, otherwise displays **Yes**.
True/False	Displays **False** if number is 0, otherwise displays **True**.
On/Off	Displays **Off** if number is 0, otherwise displays **On**.

You simply place the *Format name* in the above syntax expression, in inverted commas. You can also create your own formats with standard characters that are explained later.

As usual the best way to demonstrate something is to do it, so enter the program below into a new form.

```
Sub Form_Click ()                    ' Program EXAMPLE7.MAK
                                     ' Use of number formats
    Number = 586786.980067453        ' Set initial value

    Print "General format", Format$(Number, "General Number")
    Print "Currency format", Format$(Number, "Currency")
    Print "Fixed format", , Format$(Number, "Fixed")
    Print "Standard format", Format$(Number, "Standard")
    Print "Percent format", Format$(Number, "Percent")
    Print "Scientific format", Format$(Number, "Scientific")
    Print "Yes/No format", Format$(Number, "Yes/No")
    Print "True/False format", Format$(Number, "True/False")
    Print "On/Off format", Format$(Number, "On/Off")

End Sub
```

The result of running this code is shown below. This demonstrates the available formats quite well.

General format	586786.980067453
Currency format	£586,786.98
Fixed format	586786.98
Standard format	586,786.98
Percent format	58678698.01%
Scientific format	5.87E+05
Yes/No format	Yes
True/False format	True
On/Off format	On

User Defined Formats:

As well as the common pre-defined format types, you can build your own using a series of 'special characters'. If you need to get this detailed, we suggest you spend some time coming to terms with the Help section on the Format command, as shown on the next page.

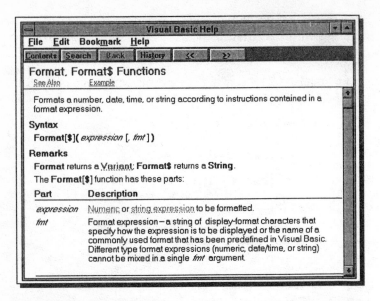

Clicking the <u>Example</u> section opens a screen of sample code on custom date formats. Try out this example yourself, use the **Copy** button and then paste the code into the Declarations section of a form, as shown below. You can then press **F5** and click the form to run the code.

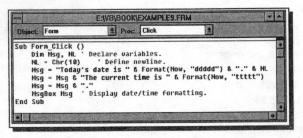

This is one of the very user friendly parts of the Visual BASIC program. The Help facility provides example code to demonstrate most of the program functions. To quickly access Help on a function, place the insertion point in the function name in the editor and press **F1**.

We will make use of other such examples as we work through this book.

6. CONTROL OF PROGRAM FLOW

Control Structures

Visual BASIC can force a section of code to be repeated by the use of the **For...Next** loop, in the same way as other standard BASICs, or by the use of the **While...Wend** loop, in the same way as other enhanced versions of BASIC. In addition to these, Visual BASIC upgrades the **While...Wend** loop with the use of the **Do** loop, which tests for a condition either at the beginning or the end of the loop.

In standard BASIC decisions are made with the use of the **If...Then** statement, while in advanced versions of it the **If...Then...Else**, **On...Goto**, and **On...Gosub** statements are also used. Visual BASIC advances these by the addition of the block **If...Then...Else...Endif** and the **Select Case** statements.

The For...Next Loop

The **For** and **Next** statements are used to mark the beginning and ending points of program loops. Any statements between the **For** and its corresponding **Next** will be executed repeatedly according to the conditions supplied by the 'control variable' within the **For** statement. An example is given below.

```
Sub Form_Click ()    ' Program EXAMPLE10.MAK
                     ' FOR....NEXT loop
For K = 1 To 5 Step 1
    Print K
Next K


End Sub
```

Within the **For** statement, the control variable K is assigned the value 1 which is increased repeatedly by the number following **Step** until it reaches 5. It thus has the values 1, 2, 3, 4 and 5. Since it cannot have these values simultaneously, a loop is formed beginning with the **For** and ending with the **Next**. The statements within the loop are executed five times, each time with a new value for K. The **Next** statement increases the value of K and causes repeated jumps to the

For statement until K exceeds its final assigned value of 5. When this happens, control passes to whatever statement follows the **Next** statement.

One of our earlier programs, EXAMPLE2.MAK, has been modified below to use a **For...Next** loop.

```
Sub Command1_Click ()        ' Program EXAMPLE11.MAK

Number = Val(InputBox$("How many numbers?"))

    For Counter = 1 To Number
        Sum = Sum + Val(InputBox$("Enter a number"))
    Next

Average = Sum / Number

Print "You entered " & Number & " numbers "
Print "Average is "; Format(Average, "Standard")
Print

End Sub
```

As it stands the above code will work as long as numerical input is entered from the keyboard. To prevent any errors the variable types should be declared as shown here. They are placed in the **(general) (declarations)** section of the form, and are hence available to any controls placed on the form.

When the program is run, Number is assigned a value from an InputBox, which is the total number of entries to be made. A **For...Next** loop is set up which loops the number of times specified in the Number variable. Within the loop, each number is read and accumulated into the variable Sum. Once the loop is completed, variable Sum holds the summation of all the numbers. The **Print** statements produce the output to the window. Note the use of the **Format** statement which forces the result variable Average to output to 2 decimal places.

54

Use of Step:

In the last example, as the **Step** modifier was equal to +1 it was omitted. If the step value desired is not equal to +1, the **Step** modifier must be included. As for example in the next small program.

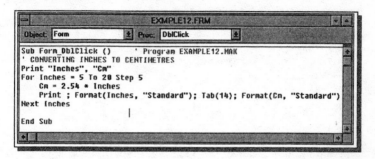

```
Sub Form_DblClick ()          ' Program EXAMPLE12.MAK
' CONVERTING INCHES TO CENTIMETRES
Print "Inches", "Cm"
For Inches = 5 To 20 Step 5
    Cm = 2.54 * Inches
    Print ; Format(Inches, "Standard"); Tab(14); Format(Cm, "Standard")
Next Inches

End Sub
```

This will convert 5, 10, 15 and 20 inches into centimetres, in other words, in steps of 5. The output should be as follows:

```
Inches      Cm
  5.00    12.70
 10.00    25.40
 15.00    38.10
 20.00    50.80
```

A negative **Step** modifier is legal in Visual BASIC. For example, the code

```
FOR J = 5 TO 1 STEP -1
    PRINT J
NEXT J
```

will print the values 5, 4, 3, 2 and 1.

For positive step values, the loop is executed so long as the control variable is less than or equal to its final value. For negative step values the loop continues as long as the control variable is greater than or equal to its final value.

Nested For...Next Loops:

For...Next statements can be nested to allow the programming of loops within loops as shown in the example below:

```
Sub Form_DblClick ()          ' Program EXMPLE13.MAK
'Nested FOR-NEXT loops

For K = 1 To 9
    For L = K To 9
        Print ; Format(L, "#");
    Next L
    Print
Next K

End Sub
```

On Running this program, two loops are set up as follows:

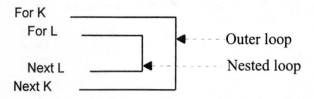

The outer loop is initialised with K=1 and, immediately, the inner, nested loop is executed 9 times. Then the control variable K is incremented by 1, so that now K=2 and the nested loop is executed 8 times. This is repeated until K is equal to 9, when the nested loop is executed only once.

The output of this program is as follows:

```
123456789
23456789
3456789
456789
56789
6789
789
89
9
```

The semicolon after the variable L in the Print statement allows output to be printed close together on the same line. However, each line of print must be terminated with a line feed (that is, it must send the computer display to the next line). This is provided here by the empty Print statement. Without it, all the numbers now appearing on different lines would be printed on the same line.

It is sometimes considered bad programming practice to exit a **For...Next** loop which has not been completed. The results may be unpredictable if you do. However, if such an exit is needed, then make sure you use the **Exit For** command (more about this later).

The Do Loop

The **Do** loop provides a method of looping through a block of statements and has several variations; it can either check the condition after or before executing the block of statements.

The Do...Loop Until Configuration:

In this configuration the **Do** marks the beginning of the loop, while the **Loop Until** marks the end. Any statements between the **Do** and its corresponding **Loop Until** will be executed repeatedly until the trailer of the **Loop Until** statement is true.

To illustrate the use of this loop configuration, enter the program below:

```
Sub Form_DblClick ()       ' Program EXMPLE14.MAK

Dim Value As Double
Dim Num As Double
Dim Percent As Double
Num = Val(InputBox$("Enter number (-1 to END) "))

Do
    Percent = Val(InputBox$("Enter % "))
    Value = Num * Percent / 100

    Print ; Format(Percent, "###.0") & " % of ";
    Print ; Format(Num, "#,###.00") & " = ";
    Print ; Format(Value, "###.00")
    Print
```

```
Num = Val(InputBox$("Enter number (-1 to END) "))

Loop Until Num < 0

End Sub
```

All statements between the **Do** and **Loop Until** lines are repeated until the trailer of **Until** is true (that is, until you type a negative value in response to the prompt "Enter number").
Note that

- In this case, the condition is checked after the statements in the block have been executed at least once. Therefore typing –1 the first time round will not end the program.
- These programs make use of the 'user defined' formats mentioned on page 51.

The Do Until...Loop Configuration:

In this configuration the loop repeats the block of statements as long as a certain condition is true. For example, the above program can be rewritten as:

```
Sub Form_DblClick ()        ' Program EXMPLE15.MAK
Dim Value As Double
Dim Num As Double
Dim Percent As Double
Num = Val(InputBox$("Enter number (-1 to END) "))

Do Until Num < 0
    Percent = Val(InputBox$("Enter % "))
    Value = Num * Percent / 100

    Print ; Format(Percent, "###.0") & " % of ";
    Print ; Format(Numr, "#,###.00") & " = ";
    Print ; Format(Value, "###.00")
    Print

    Num = Val(InputBox$("Enter number (-1 to END) "))

Loop

End Sub
```

Here, typing –1 the first time round, ends the program.

58

The Do...Loop While Configuration:

In this loop configuration, the **While** statement can be used in place of the **Until** statement, provided the relational test has been replaced by its opposite. For example the EXMPLE14 program will have to be changed to what is shown below, to produce the same logical behaviour.

Note that the relational test has been changed from less than zero (<0) to greater or equal to zero (>=0). These and other relational operators will be discussed shortly.

```
Sub Form_DblClick ()        ' Program EXMPLE16.MAK

Dim Value As Double
Dim Num As Double
Dim Percent As Double
Num = Val(InputBox$("Enter number (-1 to END) "))

Do
    Percent = Val(InputBox$("Enter % "))
    Value = Num * Percent / 100

    Print ; Format(Percent, "###.0") & " % of ";
    Print ; Format(Num, "#,###.00") & " = ";
    Print ; Format(Value, "###.00")
    Print

    Num = Val(InputBox$("Enter number (-1 to END) "))

Loop While Num >= 0

End Sub
```

The Do While...Loop Configuration:

Similarly, the EXMPLE15 program will have to be changed to

```
Sub Form_DblClick ()        ' Program EXMPLE17.MAK
Dim Value As Double
Dim Num As Double
Dim Percent As Double
Num = Val(InputBox$("Enter number (-1 to END) "))

Do While Num >= 0
    Percent = Val(InputBox$("Enter % "))
    Value = Num * Percent / 100
```

```
        Print ; Format(Percent, "###.0") & " % of ";
        Print ; Format(Numr, "#,###.00") & " = ";
        Print ; Format(Value, "###.00")
        Print

        Num = Val(InputBox$("Enter number (-1 to END) "))

    Loop

    End Sub
```

to produce the same logical behaviour as the program from
which it was derived.

The While...Wend Loop

The **While...Wend** loop is another possible configuration,
available in enhanced versions of BASIC, so included in
Visual BASIC for compatibility. It is of the general form:

```
WHILE   <relational test is true>
     { execute this }
     {   block of   }
     {  statements  }
WEND
```

This loop configuration produces the same logical behaviour
as that of the **Do While...Loop**. In order to illustrate the point,
the EXMPLE17 program is rewritten below with appropriate
changes included.

   We strongly suggest that you make the suggested
changes to these programs and verify for yourself that they
work as they should.

```
Sub Form_DblClick ()        ' Program EXMPLE18.MAK
Dim Value As Double
Dim Num As Double
Dim Percent As Double
Num = Val(InputBox$("Enter number (-1 to END) "))

While Num >= 0
    Percent = Val(InputBox$("Enter % "))
    Value = Num * Percent / 100

    Print ; Format(Percent, "###.0") & " % of ";
```

```
          Print ; Format(Numr, "#,###.00") & " = ";
          Print ; Format(Value, "###.00")
          Print

          Num = Val(InputBox$("Enter number (-1 to END) "))

Wend

End Sub
```

The If Statement

The **If** statement allows conditional program branching. To illustrate the point, edit the EXMPLE14 program to:

```
Sub Form_DblClick ()        ' Program EXMPLE19.MAK
Dim Value As Double
Dim Num As Double
Dim Percent As Double
Do
    Num = Val(InputBox$("Enter number (-1 to END) "))
    If Num <0 Then End
    Percent = Val(InputBox$("Enter % "))
    Value = Num * Percent / 100

    Print ; Format(Percent, "###.0") & " % of ";
    Print ; Format(Num, "#,###.00") & " = ";
    Print ; Format(Value, "###.00")
    Print

    Num = Val(InputBox$("Enter number (-1 to END) "))

Loop Until Num < 0

End Sub
```

When this program is run, you can now stop execution by simply entering −1 in response to the "Enter number" prompt. When the **If** statement is encountered, the value of variable Number is compared with the constant appearing after the relational operator (<). If the test condition is met, the trailer of the **If** statement is executed (in this case **End**). If, however, the test condition is not met, the next statement after the **If** statement is executed (in this case the Percent input statement).

61

Note: The inclusion of the **If...Then** statement in the form adopted above, has made the trailer of the **Loop Until** statement (Number <0) redundant; it merely acts as a device to force looping. In such cases we could use any variable as trailer. We could, for example, use

```
Loop Until False
```

This will cause repeated looping, provided the variable used as trailer is set to zero. If it has any other value, looping will halt.

Relational Operators within If Statements:
The table below shows all the relational operators allowed within an **If** statement.

_____Relational Operators_____

Symbol	Example	Meaning
=	A = B	A equal to B
<	A < B	A less than B
<=	A <= B	A less than or equal to B
>	A > B	A greater than B
>=	A >= B	A greater than or equal to B
<>	A <> B	A not equal to B

The power of the **If** statement is increased considerably by the combination of several relational expressions with the logical operators

```
And  Or  Xor  Not  Eqv  And  Imp
```

We can write the statement

```
If X>3 And M=5 Then
```

which states that only if both relational tests are met will the trailer of the **If** statement be executed.
Another example is

```
If X>3 Or M=5 Then
```

which states that when either or both relational test(s) are true, then the trailer of the **If** statement will be executed, while the statement

```
If X>3 Xor M=5 Then
```

states that when either relational test is true, but not both, then the trailer of the IF statement will be executed. Finally, the statement

```
If Not(X<12) Then
```

has the same effect as If X>=12 Then in which the relational test is the negation of that in the above.

The If...Then...Else Statement:

In many cases we have to perform an **If** statement twice over to detect which of two similar conditions is true. This is illustrated below.

```
Sub Form_DblClick ()          ' Program EXMPLE20.MAK
                              ' The two IF statements
Dim Num As Double
Num = Val(InputBox$("Enter number between 1 - 99 "))
If Num < 10 Then
    Print "One digit number"
End If
If (Num > 9) Then
    Print "Two digit number"
End If

End Sub
```

A more advanced version of the **If** statement allows both actions to be inserted in its trailer. An example of this is incorporated in the modified program below:

```
Sub Form_DblClick ()          ' Program EXMPLE21.MAK
                              ' IF..THEN..ELSE statements
Dim Num As Double
Num = Val(InputBox$("Enter number between 1 - 99 "))
If Num < 10 Then
    Print "One digit number"
```

```
Else
    Print "Two digit number"
End If

End Sub
```

Save this program under the filename *EXMPLE21.MAK* and execute it, supplying numbers between 1 and 99. Obviously, if you type in numbers greater than 99 the program will not function correctly in its present form. But assuming that you have obeyed the message and typed 50 the second **Print** statement in the trailer of the **If** statement (after the **Else**) will be executed. If the number entered was less than 10, the first **Print** statement after **Then** would be executed. The general structure of this block **If** is:

```
If  <relational test> Then
    { execute this }
    {   block of    }
    {  statements   }
    {   if true     }
Else
    { execute this }
    {   block of    }
    {  statements   }
    {   if false    }
End If
```

Note: In the above structure, no statements can follow the words **Then** and **Else**.

The ElseIf Statement:

If your programming logic requires the use of the block **If** statement to choose amongst several options by, say, using:

```
If  <relational test_1> Then
    { execute this }
    {    block     }
    {   if true    }
Else
    If  <relational test_2> Then
      { execute this }
```

64

```
     {      block    }
     {    if true   }
Else
  { execute this }
  {      block    }
  {   if false   }
End If
End If
```

then use the **ElseIf** statement to simplify the structure of your program to the following:

```
If  <relational test_1> Then
     { execute this }
     {      block    }
     {   if true   }
     ElseIf  <relational test_2> Then
       { execute this }
       {      block    }
       {   if true   }
     Else
       { execute this }
       {      block    }
       {   if false   }
End If
```

The **ElseIf** statement makes the whole structure easier to understand.

Simple Data Sorting

The program below allows us to enter two numbers, then it tests to find out which is the larger of the two and prints them in descending order. It also illustrates some of the points mentioned above.

```
Sub Form_DblClick ()        ' Program EXMPLE22.MAK
                            ' 2 number sort
Dim Num1 As Double
Dim Num2 As Double
Do
    Num1 = Val(InputBox$("Enter number [-1 to end]"))
    Num2 = Val(InputBox$("Enter second number"))
```

```
If Num1 = -1 Then
    MsgBox "Operation finished"   ' Display.
    End
ElseIf Num1 >= Num2 Then
    Print Num1, Num2
Else
    Print Num2, Num1
End If
Loop Until False

End Sub
```

The program can be stopped by entering -1 for Num1. Otherwise, Num1 is compared with Num2 and the appropriate Print statement is executed.

The sorting problem becomes more complicated, however, if instead of two numbers we introduce a third one. For two number sorting we had two possible Print statements (the number of possible permutations being 1*2=2). For three number sorting however, the total number of Print statements becomes six (the total possible permutations being equal to 1*2*3=6). With numbers A, B and C, the combinations are (A,B,C), (A,C,B), (C,A,B), (C,B,A), (B,C,A) and (B,A,C). Thus, if we were to pursue the suggested logic in dealing with the problem it would result in a very inefficient program.

Here is a way in which, with only two IF statements and one **Print** statement, the same solution to the three-number sorting problem can be achieved. It uses a different logic and it is explained here with the help of three imaginary playing cards (see Figure on the next page).

Assume that you are holding these cards in your hand and you wish to arrange them in descending order. Look at the front two (a) and arrange them so that the highest value appears in front. Now look at the back two (b) and arrange them so that the highest of these two is now in front. Obviously, if the highest card had been at the back, in the first instance, it would by now have moved to the middle position, as shown in (c), so a repeat of the whole procedure is necessary to ensure that the highest card is at the front (d).

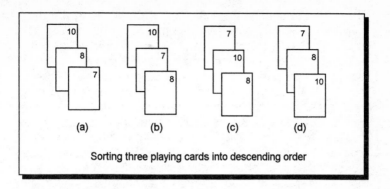

Sorting three playing cards into descending order

The program below achieves this.

```
Sub Form_DblClick ()    ' Program EXMPLE23.MAK
                        ' 3 number descending sort
Dim A As Double
Dim B As Double
Dim C As Double
Dim Temp As Double

A = Val(InputBox$("Enter first number"))
B = Val(InputBox$("Enter second number"))
C = Val(InputBox$("Enter third number"))

Do While A < B Or B < C
    If A < B Then
        Temp = A
        A = B
        B = Temp
    End If
    If B < C Then
        Temp = B
        B = C
        C = Temp
    End If
Loop
Print A, B, C

End Sub
```

67

The following actions are indicated: If the value in A is less than that in B, exchange them so that the value of A is now stored in B and the value of B is now stored in A. Note, however, that were we to put the value of B into A, we should lose the number stored in A (by overwriting). We therefore transfer the contents of A to a temporary (Temp) variable, then transfer the contents of B to A and finally transfer the contents of Temp to B. The second rotation, necessary when B is less than C, is achieved in a similar manner. The whole process is repeated (with the help of the **Do While...Loop** statement), for as long as both A is less than B, or B is less than C. Type this program into the computer under the filename EXMPLE23.MAK.

The Select Case Statement

This is a statement which allows program action to be made dependent on the value of a variable, or an expression. It is Visual BASIC's aid to writing readable programs and provides an efficient alternative to multiple **If** statements. The general form of the statement is written as follows:

```
Select Case Expression
    Case A
      { execute these }
      {  statement(s) }
    Case B To D
      { execute these }
      {  statement(s) }
    Case E,X
      { execute these }
      {  statement(s) }
    Case Else
      { execute these }
      {  statement(s) }
End Select
```

where Expression can evaluate to either a number or a string. A particular **Case** statement within the block (for example, CASE A), will be executed only if Expression evaluates to a constant or a string represented by A.

The following examples will help to illustrate the use of the **Select Case** structure. The first and simpler one, looks for input in the form of a number representing the day of the week (Monday 1, Tuesday 2, etc.). It then evaluates this DayNum variable (which is the Expression in the general format) to a constant, as follows:

```
Sub Form_DblClick ()        ' Program EXMPLE24.MAK
                            ' Using SELECT CASE

Dim DayNum As Integer

DayNum = Val(InputBox$("Enter day number (1-7) "))

Select Case DayNum
    Case 1 To 5
        Print "Working day"
    Case 6, 7
        Print "Weekend"
    Case Else
        Print "Not a day"
End Select

End Sub
```

The second example (based on that in Help), is a bit more complicated. You should make sure you understand how it works, as several keyboard entry error trapping methods are introduced.

```
Sub Form_Click ()                ' Program EXMPLE25.MAK
Dim Msg, UserInput  ' Declare variables.
Msg = "Enter a letter or number from 0 through 9."
UserInput = InputBox(Msg)    ' Get user input.
If Not IsNumeric(UserInput) Then     ' Check input type
    If Len(UserInput) <> 0 Then
        Select Case Asc(UserInput)  ' If a letter.
        Case 65 To 90    ' Must be uppercase.
            Msg = "You entered uppercase letter '"
            Msg = Msg & Chr(Asc(UserInput)) & "'."
        Case 97 To 122  ' Must be lowercase.
            Msg = "You entered lower-case letter '"
            Msg = Msg & Chr(Asc(UserInput)) & "'."
```

```
        Case Else    ' Must be something else.
            Msg = "Not a letter or number."
        End Select
    End If
Else

        Select Case CDbl(UserInput) ' If a number.
        Case 1, 3, 5, 7, 9   ' It's odd.
            Msg = UserInput & " is an odd number."
        Case 0, 2, 4, 6, 8   ' It's even.
            Msg = UserInput & " is an even number."
        Case Else    ' Out of range.
            Msg = "You entered a number outside "
            Msg = Msg & "the requested range."
        End Select
    End If
    MsgBox Msg   ' Display message.
End Sub
```

In the first **If** statement, the expression **Not IsNumeric** only accepts letters as input, not numbers. If the input is a number, control passes to the **Else** statement.

In line 7, **Asc** returns a numeric value that is the ANSI code for the letter entered (see table in next chapter). The **Case** statements then act depending on these numeric codes. The first one accepts uppercase letters (which have ANSI codes in the range 65 to 90). The second one accepts lowercase letters (which have ANSI codes in the range 97 to 122).

In line 10, the part of the expression **Chr(Asc**... changes the ANSI code back to the original character, so that it can be displayed in a message box.

The function **CDbl** in the second **Select Case** expression, explicitly converts the data type to Double precision. The following two **Case** statements select between odd and even numbers. Anything that reaches the final **Case Else** statement is neither a letter, or a number between 1 and 9, so is flagged as such.

Data Type Conversion:

The **CDbl** function in the last example explicitly converted an expression from one data type to another. Visual BASIC has 7 such functions to enable conversion to all the types of data. The syntax is

```
CType (expression)
```

Where *CType* is one of the functions from the list below and expression can be any valid string or numeric expression.

Function	*Converts to:*
CVar	Variant
CCur	Currency
CDbl	Double
CInt	Integer
CLng	Long
CSng	Single
CStr	String

You can use these data type conversion functions to ensure that the result of a calculation is expressed as a particular data type rather than the normal data type of the result.

Exiting Block Structures

If, for any reason, you require to exit a loop, a function or a procedure prematurely (for example when a data search for a match is successful), then use one of the following:

```
Exit Do
Exit For
Exit Function
Exit Sub
```

the first two being used to exit loops, and the last, to exit functions and procedures.

71

7. STRINGS AND ARRAYS

String Variables

In Visual BASIC, string variables can be distinguished from numeric variables by including the $ tag after their name, or more usually, by declaring them as such in a Dimension statement, such as:

```
Dim A AS String
```

By default, a string variable has a flexible length. It gets longer, or shorter, as you assign different data to it. To fix its length you can add the required size to the statement:

```
Dim A AS String * 25
```

In this case A will always be allocated 25 characters of storage space. If it does not need this length it will be 'padded' with trailing spaces. If the data it holds is longer than 25 characters it will be truncated (and some will be lost).

If a variable is not declared in a program it takes the default **Variant** type, which is a special data type that can contain numeric, string, date, or currency data.

As with numbers, strings can be assigned to variables in several ways. For example, the code below assigns a string to the variable named A$ and then prints A$ to the current window.

```
A$="ABC123"
Print A$
```

When the code is run, Visual BASIC outputs

```
ABC123
```

ANSI Character Codes

Visual BASIC assigns a numeric code to each character on the keyboard, according to the ANSI (American National Standards Institute) code, as shown in the tables overleaf. Thus, each letter of the alphabet is assigned a numeric value. The first 128 characters (0 - 127) are common with the ASCII set used in most DOS applications.

_____Table 1 of ANSI Conversion Codes_____

0	●	32	[space]	64	@	96	`
1	●	33	!	65	A	97	a
2	●	34	"	66	B	98	b
3	●	35	#	67	C	99	c
4	●	36	$	68	D	100	d
5	●	37	%	69	E	101	e
6	●	38	&	70	F	102	f
7	●	39	'	71	G	103	g
8	* *	40	(	72	H	104	h
9	* *	41	)	73	I	105	i
10	* *	42	*	74	J	106	j
11	●	43	+	75	K	107	k
12	●	44	,	76	L	108	l
13	* *	45	-	77	M	109	m
14	●	46	.	78	N	110	n
15	●	47	/	79	O	111	o
16	●	48	0	80	P	112	p
17	●	49	1	81	Q	113	q
18	●	50	2	82	R	114	r
19	●	51	3	83	S	115	s
20	●	52	4	84	T	116	t
21	●	53	5	85	U	117	u
22	●	54	6	86	V	118	v
23	●	55	7	87	W	119	w
24	●	56	8	88	X	120	x
25	●	57	9	89	Y	121	y
26	●	58	:	90	Z	122	z
27	●	59	;	91	[	123	{
28	●	60	<	92	\	124		
29	●	61	=	93	]	125	}
30	●	62	>	94	^	126	~
31	●	63	?	95	_	127	●

●   Characters not supported by Microsoft Windows.

* *   Values 8, 9, 10, and 13, above, convert to backspace, tab, linefeed, and carriage return respectively and can be used in programs to create these actions.

Table 2 of ANSI Conversion Codes

128	●	160	[space]	192	À	224	à
129	●	161	¡	193	Á	225	á
130	●	162	¢	194	Â	226	â
131	●	163	£	195	Ã	227	ã
132	●	164	¤	196	Ä	228	ä
133	●	165	¥	197	Å	229	å
134	●	166	¦	198	Æ	230	æ
135	●	167	§	199	Ç	231	ç
136	●	168	¨	200	È	232	è
137	●	169	©	201	É	233	é
138	●	170	ª	202	Ê	234	ê
139	●	171	«	203	Ë	235	ë
140	●	172	¬	204	Ì	236	ì
141	●	173	-	205	Í	237	í
142	●	174	®	206	Î	238	î
143	●	175	¯	207	Ï	239	ï
144	●	176	°	208	Ð	240	ð
145	●	177	±	209	Ñ	241	ñ
146	●	178	²	210	Ò	242	ò
147	●	179	³	211	Ó	243	ó
148	●	180	´	212	Ô	244	ô
149	●	181	µ	213	Õ	245	õ
150	●	182	¶	214	Ö	246	ö
151	●	183	·	215	×	247	÷
152	●	184	¸	216	Ø	248	ø
153	●	185	¹	217	Ù	249	ù
154	●	186	º	218	Ú	250	ú
155	●	187	»	219	Û	251	û
156	●	188	¼	220	Ü	252	ü
157	●	189	½	221	Ý	253	ý
158	●	190	¾	222	Þ	254	þ
159	●	191	¿	223	ß	255	ÿ

Note: The codes within the range 128 to 255 above contain a series of special characters that are not on the standard keyboard. These include international and accented letters, fractions and currency symbols.

When strings appear in an **If** statement, they are compared character by character from left to right on the basis of the ANSI values until a difference is found. For example, if a character in a position in StringA has a higher ANSI code than the character in the same position in StringB, then StringA is greater than StringB. If all the characters in the same positions are identical but one string has more characters than the other, the longer string is the greater of the two. Thus, strings of letters can be placed easily in alphabetical order and sorted lists of names, etc., are possible.

String Functions
In the statements given so far, the string variables have been considered in their entirety. We shall now introduce some functions which give access to any character within a given string and hence allow manipulation of that string.

Left and Left$ Functions:
These both return a number of characters from the left of a string argument. The function is used as follows:

```
Left[$](StringA, n)
```

and will return the leftmost n characters of StringA. When used without the $ suffix, **Left** returns a Variant; whereas **Left$** returns a String. In most cases you are probably better off adding the $ and declaring all your string variables as such.

Right and Right$ Functions:
These work in exactly the same way as the **Left[$]** functions, but they return the rightmost characters of the specified string.

Mid and Mid$ Functions:
In the same way, these return a Variant or String from part of a source string, as follows:

```
Mid[$](StringA, Start[, Length])
```

Where Start and Length are numbers. In this case the string with Length number of characters and beginning at position Start of StringA will be returned.

If Length is omitted the **Mid[$]** function returns all the characters from the start position to the end of the string.

Other String Functions:

There are a few more functions that help with string manipulation, most of which will be demonstrated in later examples.

The **Len(**StringA**)** function is used to find the number of characters in StringA.

The **InStr(**[Start,] StringA, StringB**)** function returns the location of StringB in StringA, optionally beginning the search Start characters into the string. If Start is omitted the search will begin at the first character. This function is very useful for locating spaces between words in a string.

Space$(Num**)** will create a string with Num spaces in it, and **String$(**Num, "X"**)** will create a string consisting of Num characters of type X. If a number is used for X the ANSI code character will be used. The first is useful, with no number to place spaces between words being built in a string expression, the second for building lines with graphic type characters.

Ucase$(StringA**)** and **Lcase$(**StringA**)** convert all the characters in StringA to upper, or lower, case respectively. An example of their use is to convert keyboard entry characters before testing for the entry. Otherwise you would have to test for both upper and lower case letters.

The best way to understand these functions is by entering

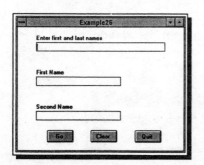

and playing with an example; so build the Form shown here. This small program does not really serve any great purpose. It expects you to enter your First and last names into the top text box **separated by a space**. Clicking the **Go** button places the two parts of the name into their respective text boxes. The **Clear** button resets the boxes and **Quit** exits the program.

The form has 3 Text boxes, with a Label placed above each, and 3 Command buttons, as shown. You may have to go back to the earlier chapters if you need help setting these up. Set the following object Properties as shown, but leave the others with the default settings.

Object	*Property*	*Setting*
Command1	Caption	Go
	Default*	True
	Name	ComGo
Command2	Caption	Clear
	Name	ComClear
Command3	Caption	Quit
	Cancel*	True
	Name	ComQuit
Label1	Caption	Enter first and last names
Label2	Caption	First Name
Label3	Caption	Last Name
Text1	TabIndex	0
	Text	Cleared
Text2	Text	Cleared
Text3	Text	Cleared

*   See end of example for more explanation.

When you have finished the above Property changes, double click the background of the form and enter the declaration statement below into the **(general) (declarations)** box. This allows the variable Usr$ to be used from any of the form's commands.

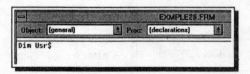

Then double-click the Text1 box and enter the following code, making sure it is entered into the Change procedure code window. This will then be actioned whenever the text entered into the box is changed at run time.

```
Sub Text1_Change ()
    Usr$ = Text1.Text
End Sub
```

The main code to work the program is next entered in the code window of the Go Command button.

```
Sub ComGo_Click ()

Dim LWord, Msg, Rword, SpcPos   ' Declare variables.

    SpcPos = InStr(1, Usr$, " ")  ' Find the space.
    If SpcPos Then
        LWord = Left(Usr$, SpcPos - 1)
        Rword = Right(Usr$, Len(Usr$) - SpcPos)
        Text2.Text = UCase$(LWord) ' First name
        Text3.Text = UCase$(Rword) ' Last name
    Else
        Msg = "You didn't enter two words."
        MsgBox Msg  ' Display error message.
        Text1.Text = "" ' Clear text box
        Text1.SetFocus  ' Place insertion point in box
    End If

End Sub
```

In the Click procedure code window of the Clear Command button, enter the following code which clears the text boxes and places the insertion point in the first, ready for input.

```
Sub ComClear_Click ()

    Text1.Text = ""
    Text1.SetFocus
    Text2.Text = ""
    Text3.Text = ""

End Sub
```

Last of all, place the one word of code in the Quit Command button code window as follows:

```
Sub ComQuit_Click ()
    End 'Close program
End Sub
```

The logic of the code 'behind' the Go button should be fairly easy to follow. Four local variables are first declared, which are only used in this subroutine. The **Instr** function then looks for a space (" ") in the entered text held in the variable Usr$ (short for User Input).

If a space is found, the lines under the **If** statement are actioned. The first and last names are cut out of the Usr$ string and then converted to upper case.

If no space character is found, the **Else** statements are actioned. An error message is placed on the screen, the input text box is cleared and the focus is placed back into it to receive correct input.

Two of the Properties set in this example need more comment. The Quit Command button property *Cancel* was set to True. This controls the action of the <Esc> key in the program. With this setting pressing the <Esc> key is the same as clicking this button.

The Go Command button property *Default* was also set to True. This controls the action of the <Enter> key. Pressing this key then has the same effect as clicking the Go button.

String Conversion Functions

There are four additional string functions in Visual BASIC:

```
Asc( ), Chr$( ), Str$( ) and Val( )
```

Examples of the use of these functions are given next.

ANSI Conversion:

The use of the **Asc** function in the statement

```
N = Asc("ABCD")
```

will return the ANSI code for the first character of the string enclosed in the brackets of the function. In this case, 65 will be returned (see Table on ANSI Conversion Codes). The function name ASC actually refers to ASCII code conversion as used in previous DOS versions of BASIC. But all the usual keyboard codes are the same in both codes, so the name has been kept in Visual BASIC to maintain compatibility with code written for earlier versions.

Character Conversion:
The use of the **Chr$** function in the statement

```
C$ = Chr$(66)
```

will return the ANSI character that corresponds to the value of the argument, in this case the letter B. The value of the argument must lie between 0 and 255.

String Conversion:
The use of the **Str$** function in the statement

```
S$ = Str$(X)
```

will convert the value of the argument into a string. X is a numeric variable which might be the result of a calculation. In this case, if X had the value of 98.56, say, then S$ becomes equal to "98.56".

Value of String:
If R$ represents a string given by

```
R$ = "3.123E12 metres"
```

then the statement

```
X = Val(R$)
```

will return the value of the string up to the first non-numeric character, in this case 3.123E+12. If the string begins with a non-numeric character then the value 0 is returned.

String Concatenation:
BASIC allows the concatenation (joining together) of strings. We shall illustrate this facility by considering the following program in which the computer asks you to enter your surname first followed by your first name. It then

concatenates the two (first name first followed by surname with a space in between) and prints the result which is held in string variable X$.

```
Sub Form_Click ()   ' Program EXAMPLE27.MAK
    Dim SName, FName, WName
    SName = InputBox$("Enter SURNAME please")
    FName = InputBox$("Enter FIRST NAME please")
    WName = UCase$(FName) + Space$(1) + UCase$(SName)

    Print "HELLO " & WName

End Sub
```

As it stands, the program is rather trivial. However, using concatenation together with some of the string functions mentioned earlier, can result in a somewhat more spectacular result. To illustrate this, delete the Print statement of the above program and replace it with the following lines to the program:

```
FontName = "Courier New"   ' Program EXAMPLE28.MAK
FontSize = 10

L = Len(WName)
If L > 22 Then
    WName = UCase$(Left$(FName, 1) + ". " + SName)
    L = Len(WName)
End If
For I = 1 To L
    Print Mid$(WName, I, 1);
    If I = 1 Then Print " "; WName;
    If I = L Then Print " "; WName;
    Print Tab(L + 4); Mid$(WName, I, 1)
Next I
```

Run the program and supply it with your full name (surname first). What you would see in the form window, if your name was JOHN BROWN, is shown on the next page. This would not work properly without the first line above, which sets the printing font to Courier New which is not proportional.

```
J  JOHN  BROWN  J
O              O
H              H
N              N

B              B
R              R
O              O
W              W
N  JOHN  BROWN  N
```

Note that the program has worked out the length of your full name and allowed enough space between the two vertical columns to write it horizontally on the first and last rows.

Now Run the program again, but this time type in a really long name, say CHRISTOPHER VERYLONGFELLOW. Can you work out from the program lines and the output on your screen what has happened? Try it.

Arrays

Some people find difficulty understanding the concept of arrays in programming. An array is a set of sequentially indexed elements of the same type and name, with each element having a unique index number to identify it. Changes made to one element of an array do not affect the other elements.

An array can only store data of the same type. Of course, if the array data type is Variant, then numerical, string and date/time data can all be stored in the same array.

String Arrays:

A number of strings can be stored under a common name in a string array. Let us assume that we have four names, e.g., SMITH, JONES, BROWN and WILSON that we want to store in a string array. In Visual BASIC, whenever an array is to be used in a program, you must declare your intention to do so. There are several ways of doing this. One is to place a **Dim**ension statement, like the one on the next page, into the **(general) (declarations)** section of a form. This, dimensions the array Names() with the elements 1 to 4, and allows the array to be used from any of the form's commands.

```
Dim Names(1 To 4) As String
```

Enter this line into the declarations section of a new project form and then type the following code into the Click procedure:

```
Sub Form_Click ()   ' Program EXAMPLE29.MAK
                    ' Use of a string array
    Dim I As Integer
    Names(1) = "SMITH"   ' Load array
    Names(2) = "JONES"
    Names(3) = "BROWN"
    Names(4) = "WILSON"

    For I = 1 To 4
        Print "Names("; I; ")",
    Next I
    Print
    For I = 1 To 4
        Print Names(I),
    Next I
    Print
End Sub
```

When run, this program demonstrates how the 4 elements of the array Names() can be manipulated by using the index number of each element in your code. Any reference to an array name within a program must be of the form

```
Names(I)
```

Another way of dimensioning this array with 4 elements is:

```
Dim Names(4) As String
```

However, the element numbers in this case would be 0 to 3, as unless the range is implicitly declared it starts, by default, from 0. You can, if you want, force the lower 'bound' to 1 by placing the line

```
Option Base 1
```

in the declarations section of your form.

A simple way to visualise a string array is as follows:

SMITH	JONES	BROWN	WILSON

The four names are stored in a common box which has four compartments (or elements), each compartment containing one name. Thus, Names(2) refers to the 2nd element of string array Names(), and Names(4) to the 4th element.

Subscripted Numeric Variables

Array variables are often called subscripted variables and they permit the representation of many quantities with one variable name. A particular quantity is indicated, as we saw above, by writing a subscript in parentheses after the variable name. So an array allows you to use a single variable name for a complete list of related data. Items from the list are located by their index (or subscript) number, which can be referred to as a number, or an expression that results in a number. In Visual BASIC an array may have up to 60 dimensions, each one represented by a different subscript.

The elements of a one-dimensional array can be represented as follows:

    A(0)   A(1)   A(2)   A(3)   A(4)

while those of a two-dimensional array as:

    A(0,0)   A(0,1)   A(0,2)   A(0,3)
    A(1,0)   A(1,1)   A(1,2)   A(1,3)
    A(2,0)   A(2,1)   A(2,2)   A(2,3)

The first of the two subscripts refers to the row number, running from 0 to the maximum number of declared rows, and the second subscript to the column number, running from 0 to the maximum number of declared columns.

A three-dimensional array can be thought of as stacked two-dimensional arrays with the third subscript, running from 0 to the maximum height of the stack. More complex structures follow the same procedures.

As with string arrays, numerical arrays must be declared prior to their use, either with a **Dim** statement placed in the declarations section of a form or module, with a **Global** statement placed in the declarations section of a module, or with a **Static** statement placed in the procedure.

When declared with:

Global   an array is available to any form or module contained in a project.

Dim   an array is available to any procedure on the form or module on which it is placed.

Static   an array is available only within the procedure in which it is declared.

The form of the statement is shown below:

```
Dim X(15), Y(3,5), Z(3,5,4)
Global X(15), Y(3,5), Z(3,5,4)
Static X(15), Y(3,5), Z(3,5,4)
```

where array X() has been declared to be a one-dimensional array with a maximum of 16 elements (don't forget the zero'th element), array Y(,) has been declared as a two-dimensional array of 4 rows and 6 columns, and array Z(,,) as a three-dimensional array of 4 rows and 6 columns stacked 5 deep. The number of arrays that can be declared simultaneously is dependent only on the available memory in your computer. Don't forget that multi-dimensional arrays can very quickly eat into your available memory.

Static and Dynamic Arrays

Visual BASIC allows you to assign a portion of memory for array use in two different ways. These are:

Static arrays   When the declaration is made with subscripted variables, for example DIM Year(1980 TO 2000) or DIM Aname(15)

Dynamic arrays   When the declaration is made with empty subscript brackets, for example

Dim Year() or Dim Aname()

Static array memory is always the same size for each run of the program and cannot be used for any other purpose.

Dynamic memory is allocated during run time and the space may vary for each run of the program. Dynamic memory can be freed at any time for other use with the statement

```
Erase Array_name
```

This command also reinitialises the elements of fixed arrays as well as freeing dynamic array storage space.

Before your program can refer to the dynamic array again, it must re-declare the array variable's dimensions using a **ReDim** statement. However, although dynamic arrays are memory efficient, accessing values held in them may be slightly slower that accessing values held in static arrays.

There are two main error messages which relate to the use of arrays. These are:

```
Subscript out of range
Overflow
```

The first error occurs if an attempt is made to use an array element that is outside the declared dimension, or if an attempt has been made to dimension the array with a negative number of elements. The second error occurs if an attempt is made to use an array for which there is no room in the computer's memory.

As an example of array usage we will build a small stocktaking program. After you have studied it, enter the code as EXMPLE30.MAK.

First declare two arrays in the declarations section of a new project form as follows:

```
Dim Item(4) As String
Dim Stock(4, 2) As Double
```

Then enter the following code into the Click procedure of the form. Note the use of the colon (:) to separate multiple statements on a line. You could enter all the Print statements together on one line if you prefer.

```
Sub Form_click ()    ' Program EXAMPLE30.MAK
                     ' Stocktaking program
Dim I As Integer, Xname As String
Item(1) = "INK ERASER"        'Load data into arrays
Stock(1, 1) = 200: Stock(1, 2) = .1
Item(2) = "PENCIL ERASER"
Stock(2, 1) = 320: Stock(2, 2) = .15
Item(3) = "TYPING ERASER"
Stock(3, 1) = 25: Stock(3, 2) = .25
Item(4) = "CORRECTION FLUID"
Stock(4, 1) = 150: Stock(4, 2) = .5

Do
    Xname = InputBox$("Which item? 'END' to finish")
    If UCase$(Xname) = "END" Then End
    For I = 1 To 4
        If UCase$(Xname) = Left$(Item(I), 3) Then
            Print Item(I); "  ";
            Print  Stock(I, 1) & " in stock @ ";
            Print Format(Stock(I, 2), "Currency");
            Print " each."
        End If
    Next I
Loop Until False

End Sub
```

When run, the Input Box will only accept an entry whose first
three letters are the same as one of the items entered into
the Item() array.

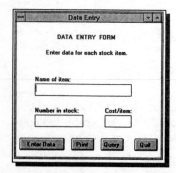

The last example included all
the data for the arrays in the
code. This is not always
convenient, so the next one
has a front-end data entry
form and the user can enter
any suitable data at run time.

Form1, shown here, has
been given the *Name*
property 'Data Entry'.

It has 3 Text Boxes, 4 Command Buttons and several Labels. Open a new project (EXMPLE31.MAK) with 2 forms and a Code Module. This is the first time we have used more than one form. Don't panic, simply click the New Form and New Module icons on the Toolbar. The second form will be used purely as a window to hold our print output, and the module will be used for global declarations of our arrays.

We will leave it to you to build the Form1 entry form on your own. The code for the various objects is shown in the **File**, **Save Text** format.

First the declarations placed in the new code module:

```
Option Base 1
Global Item(10) As String
Global Stock(10, 2) As Double
```

Then the code for the 4 command buttons, which have been renamed, as shown below, to Enter, Print, Query and Quit.

```
Sub Enter_Click ()        ' Program EXAMPLE31.MAK
                ' Improved stocktaking program
Static Counter  As Integer
    If Counter < 1 Then Counter = 1
    Item(Counter) = Text1.Text
    Stock(Counter, 1) = Val(Text2.Text)
    Stock(Counter, 2) = Val(Text3.Text)
    Counter = Counter + 1
    Text1.Text = ""
    Text2.Text = ""
    Text3.Text = ""
    Text1.SetFocus
End Sub


Sub Print_Click ()
Form2.Show
For I = 1 To 10
Form2.Print Item(I), Stock(I, 1),
Form2.Print Format(Stock(I, 2), "Currency")
Next I
End Sub
```

```
Sub Query_Click ()
Dim I As Integer, Xname As String
Do
    Form2.Show
    Msg = "Which item? 'END' to finish"
    Xname = InputBox$(Msg,"Data Query",,7000,5000)
    If UCase$(Xname) = "END" Then End
    For I = 1 To 10
    If UCase$(Xname) = UCase$(Left$(Item(I), 3)) Then
        Form2.Print Item(I); "  ";
        Form2.Print Stock(I, 1) & " in stock @ ";
        Form2.Print Format(Stock(I, 2), "Currency");
        Form2.Print " each."
    End If
    Next I
Loop Until False
End Sub

Sub Quit_Click ()
    End
End Sub
```

You should, by now, be able to follow this code quite easily. Remember that if you forget the correct syntax for a command, simply select it in the editing window and press **F1**. As it stands the program will accept 10 sets of data, but would be easy to modify.

The **Static** declaration allows the variable 'Counter' to maintain its value; without this it would be re-set each time the Sub was run.

The statement 'Form2.**Show**' opens the window Form2 and the Print statements have to be prefixed with 'Form2.' to force printing onto this window (otherwise it will run behind the features on Form1.

The **InputBox$()** statement has a title as well as X and Y co-ordinates to force the box to the lower right portion of the screen. Otherwise it opens over the Form2 printing window. You must use all the positioning commas, as shown, to get these to work.

8. MORE ON CONTROLS

In Chapter 3, we briefly described the main controls available in Visual BASIC, but so far we have not actually used some of them. We have concentrated more on the fundamentals of the programming language itself.

Perhaps the easiest way to come to terms with the other controls is to study how the sample program CONTROLS.MAK works. This was found in our set-up in the VB\SAMPLES\CONTROLS directory. Load this project and set up your screen as shown below. Here, we have opened the MAIN.FRM by selecting it in the Project window and then clicked the **View Form** button.

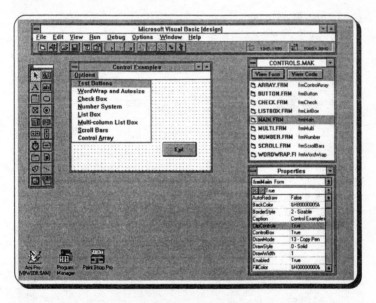

This form has an **Exit** button, which you should be very familiar with, and a menu item, shown opened above. The menu gives access to the other forms which make up this project.

If you double-click the MAIN.FRM window and open the **Object** drop down list you will see reference to all the menu code windows. The screen dump overleaf shows this list and a typical Procedure code.

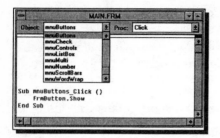

In each case, the code simply opens the relevant form window using the **Show** statement.

This is a very easy way to transfer control around the program, and we will look at how to set up menus a little later on. In the meantime, run the program and move between the various options. You will be amazed at what can be produced in Visual BASIC with very little in the way of code.

Control Buttons

The Test Buttons routine shows a traffic light which changes from green to amber and then red when a button is clicked.

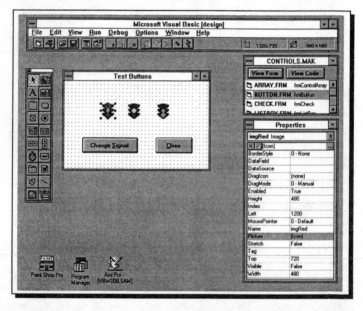

On close inspection the form actually has three picture icons, with different colours active, superimposed on top of each other, with only one having its *Visible* property set as True.

92

Clicking the **Change Signal** button calls the ChangeSignal procedure shown here, which steps through the colour sequence in the right order setting only one as *Visible* at a time.

Note that ChangeSignal is a Sub procedure not related to any particular object action (such as clicking the mouse). It can be called from anywhere on the current form and is placed in the **(general)** procedure section.

Before we leave the Buttons part of the program, look at the code that is activated by clicking the **Close** button.

```
Unload Me
```

As its name suggests, this closes the active window and wipes its display from the screen. In this program control returns to the MAIN.FRM opening window.

Check Boxes

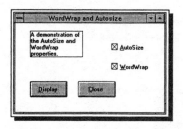

Check boxes are used on the WORDWRAP form which also gives a clear demonstration of how the *AutoSize* and *WordWrap* properties of a Label work.

A long caption has been entered into a Label of specific size. Clicking the two check boxes selects whether the *AutoSize* and *WordWrap* properties of a Label are to be set or not. When the program is run, clicking the **Display** button sets the two Label properties, and the result can be seen in the display. The code behind the **Display** button is:

```
Sub cmdDisplay_Click ()
' Reset the example
```

```
        lblDisplay.AutoSize = False
        lblDisplay.WordWrap = False
        lblDisplay.Width = 1695
        lblDisplay.Height = 255
' Check for WordWrap and Autosize
        If chkWordWrap.Value = 1 Then
            lblDisplay.WordWrap = True
        End If
        If chkAutoSize.Value = 1 Then
            lblDisplay.AutoSize = True
        End If
End Sub
```

This, first sets the *AutoSize* and *WordWrap* settings of the label to False, sizes the label and then looks at the Check box settings. If either is selected, its *Value* property will be '1' and the above procedure will set the Label property to 'True'.

A Check box displays an X when selected and, as we have seen, is used to give the user True/False or Yes/No options. They are usually used in groups to display multiple choices, any of which can be selected.

Check boxes and Option buttons function similarly but only one Option button in a group can be selected.

To display text next to the Check box, enter it into the *Caption* property of the box.

The *Value* property determines the state of a Check box, as used in the above program - the available settings being:

0 is Unchecked, the default setting.
1 is Checked, or selected.
2 is Greyed (dimmed), unavailable.

Option Buttons

An Option button displays an option that can be turned on or off. They are used to display multiple choices from which the user can select only one. You can group option buttons by drawing them inside a frame or a picture box, or directly onto a form. All those placed directly onto a form are treated as a separate group.

The Number System example in CONTROLS.MAK uses Option buttons to make a choice between three options.

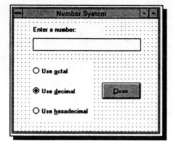

The three Option buttons shown, form a group on the form, so only one of them can be set at any one time.

To set a default option (in this case **Use decimal**, set the *Value* property of that option to True.

In this example, when a number is entered into the Text box it is screened and given the variable name of CurrentNum. If you click the **Use octal** option button, the following code will be actioned

```
Sub optOctButton_Click ()
    txtNumber.Text = Oct(CurrentNum)
End Sub
```

which places the Octal format of the number into the Text box.

Combo and List Boxes

These are both used to display a list of items from which the user can choose one. The list can be scrolled if it has more items than can be displayed at one time. A list box only allows a choice from an existing list, whereas a Combo box has a Text box feature at the top of the list, into which you can type a new choice.

Dependant on the *Style* property, *Text* determines the text that is contained in the text edit area of a Combo box, or the selected item in the list box. This property is read-only at both design and run time.

The *Style* property sets the type of combo box drawn:

0 - Dropdown Combo Includes a drop-down list and an edit area. The user can select from the list, or type into the edit area.

1 - Simple Combo Includes an edit area and a list that is always displayed. The user can select from the list, or type into the edit area. By default, this type is sized so that none of the list shows. Increasing the *Height* property will show more of the list.

2 - Dropdown List   This style only allows selection from the drop-down list.

If the *Sorted* property is set to 'True', all items in a list are automatically sorted alphabetically at run time. The default setting, 'False', does not sort a list.

A Simple Telephone List:

The following small program shows how a Combo box, or

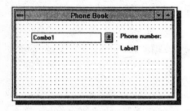

List box, can be loaded at run time, and usefully used. It represents a telephone 'directory' with, as it stands, only room for 5 entries, but it could very easily be extended.

The form, shown here in Design mode, has a Combo box and two labels. The only reason a List box is not used is that it takes up much more room on the form.

Set the *Style* property of the Combo to **0 - Dropdown Combo** and the *Caption* properties as shown.

We will use two arrays, one to hold the names and the other, the telephone numbers, so place the following in the general declarations section of the form.

```
Dim SName(0 To 4)            ' Dimension arrays.
Dim TelNum(0 To 4)
```

The main body of the code loads the arrays with data and then places the names in the Combo list. This is carried out when the program starts up, so the code is placed as a Form_Load procedure.

```
Sub Form_Load ()             ' Program EXMPLE32.MAK
    Dim I                    ' Declare variable.
    AutoSize = True
```

```
SName(0) = "Dean, Jim" ' Enter data into arrays.
SName(1) = "Woolgatherer, Larry"
SName(2) = "Smith, Archibold"
SName(3) = "Splurg, Andrew"
SName(4) = "Bloggs, Alfred"
TelNum(0) = "0173 789987"
TelNum(1) = "54645"
TelNum(2) = "010 45 678123"
TelNum(3) = "01209 311887"
TelNum(4) = "789456"

For I = 0 To 4        ' Add names to list.
    Combo1.AddItem SName(I)
Next I
Combo1.ListIndex = 0  'Display first list item
End Sub
```

You could obviously substitute more meaningful data in the above if you wanted. All that remains now is to place a line of code behind the Combo so that the telephone number of the person selected in the List shows in the main Label box.

```
Sub Combo1_Click ()
            ' Display corresponding Number for name.
    Label1.Caption = TelNum(Combo1.ListIndex)
End Sub
```

When you have entered the code and are happy with the way it works, try changing the *Style* property of the Combo box to see the different types available. With the above code, whatever you do, don't try sorting the list with the *Sorted* property. The array indices would not then be the same and incorrect phone numbers would be displayed!

As we saw in the previous example, to display items in a combo or list box, you use the **AddItem** statement. To remove items, you would use **RemoveItem** in the same way.

The *ListIndex* property determines the index of the currently selected item in a list; this cannot be used at design time. The *ListCount* property (also not available at design time) specifies the number of items in the list. The statement

```
Combo1.ListCount
```

would return the number of items in the list of Combo1.

The Timer Control

Visual BASIC's timer, which is invisible to the user at run time, is used for background processing. A Timer Control runs code at regular intervals by causing a Timer event, which occurs when a pre-set interval of time has elapsed. The timing frequency is set in the control's *Interval* property, which specifies the length of time in milliseconds. The other

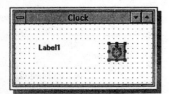

main Timer property is the *Enabled* property. When this is set to True with the *Interval* property greater than zero, the Timer event waits for the period specified in the *Interval* property.

A very simple digital clock can be programmed by placing a Timer and a Label on a form as shown here. The code required is minimal.

```
Sub Form_Load ()
    Timer1.Interval = 1000   ' Set timer interval.
End Sub


Sub Timer1_Timer ()
    Label1.Caption = Time    ' Update time display.
End Sub
```

In the first procedure, the Timer *Interval* property is set to 1000 milliseconds, or 1 second. In the second, the Timer is set to call the Visual BASIC Time function after every 1 second interval, the Label *Caption* being updated every second with the computer system time.

When run, a digital clock is operational in the window. By changing the form and label properties you can customise this 'clock' with alarms, colours and fonts, etc.

Building a Menu Bar

To make creating menus for your windows reasonably easy, Visual BASIC has a Menu Design window in which you can create custom menus and define their properties. Before we can demonstrate this procedure you need a program with a form that needs a menu bar. We suggest you create the following small program.

98

A Simple VAT Calculator:

Appendix A contains all the code, complete with object properties, for you to build the small program named VATCALC.MAK, that asks for number input and then calculates and displays VAT information, as shown below.

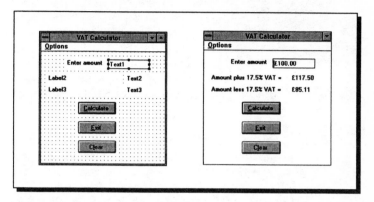

The main form, **frmVatCalc** is shown on the left above in Design mode, and on the right in Run mode. The Label *Caption* and Text box *Text* properties are shown named above so that you can see where they are. These must all be deleted (in the Properties window) before the program will work properly!

You should have no problem building this form from what we have covered so far, except for the Menu bar. This has

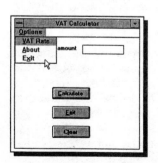

only one item (**Options**) on the main bar, and three sub-menu items when it is opened, as shown here.

Governments have a habit of increasing tax levels at regular intervals, so the first menu item allows the user to change the VAT rate (from the present 17.5%).

The **Exit** item is not really necessary, as this is already taken care of with a Command button, but it is better to have too many ways out, than not enough.

The **About** menu item opens another form and displays some information about the program.

This is included to demonstrate some other techniques and is, in fact, based on a similar form which you will find in the sample program TEXTEDIT.MAK. It is a demonstration of a fully working text editor and we will use this project again in a later chapter.

You should find it in the VB\SAMPLES\MENUS directory of your system.

The Menu Design Window:

With the main **frmVatCalc** form selected, choose **Menu Design** from the **Window** menu, or use <Ctrl+M>, or click the toolbar icon shown here. This will open the following window. In the **Caption** text

box, you type the menu item caption that you want displayed on the menu bar. In our case you type &Options.

The ampersand (&) character will give the user keyboard access to this menu item. At run time, the next letter is underlined, and the menu can be accessed by pressing Alt plus the access key, <Alt+O>.

If you had wanted to create a separator bar in your menu, you could type a single hyphen (-) in this box.

In the **Name** box, type the control name that will be used to refer to this menu item in code, in our case **mnuOption**.

Leave the other options in the Design Window at their default settings and click the **Next** button. Next type **&VAT Rate** in the **Caption** text box and **mnuVATRate** in the **Name**

box. Now click the Right Arrow on the Window button bar to make this menu item secondary to the first, as shown here, and press **Next**. Add the other two menu items as follows:

Caption	Name
&About	mnuAbout
E&xit	mnuExit

The Menu Design Window should now look like ours, shown alongside. Pressing **OK** will close the window and place the menu bar on your form.

Using the left and right arrows you can have up to four levels of sub-menus. The up and down arrows change the position of a menu item in the list box.

We did not use the other features in the Design Window, but their functions are:

Index Type an index number to control the position of a menu item within a control array.

Shortcut Use to assign a shortcut key to a menu item by selecting a key from the drop-down list.

WindowList Select if you want the current menu control to include the name of open MDI child forms (outside the scope of this book).

HelpContextID Enter a unique number if you plan to provide a context-sensitive Help topic.

C̲hecked	Select if you want a check mark to appear at the left of a menu item to indicate that the control is turned on.
E̲nabled	Select if you want the menu item to initially respond to events. Clear the box if you want the menu item to be unavailable (greyed on the menu) to be enabled later in your code.
V̲isible	Select if you want the menu item to appear on the menu.

The menu items you created, although visible, will not do anything until you write code for them (as with other controls). In Design mode, if you click on a Menu Bar item the sub-menu will open, but if you click on a sub-menu item its code window will open. As an example, the code below is placed behind the **V̲AT Rate** sub-menu item.

```
Sub mnuVATRate_Click ()
' Get new VAT rate from user.
NVATRate = Val(InputBox$("Enter new VAT rate"))
VATRate = NVATRate
End Sub
```

This opens an Input Box that requires a new VAT rate to be entered. The other code for the two forms and all their controls is given in Appendix A.

The **Sub** mnuAbout_Click procedure loads the contents into the form named frmAbout with the statement

```
frmAbout.Show 1
```

The Show command displays a form. The following integer (1 or 0) sets the style as modal or modeless. When a form is modal, it must be removed with the **UnLoad** command before the program can continue. (Done in the **Sub** cmdAbout_Click procedure). The default is modeless, which lets the form stay active, and a 0 is not actually necessary.

Make sure you study the comments in the code, as they explain several of the features of the program. The rest we will leave to you.

9. FUNCTIONS & PROCEDURES

Standard Mathematical Functions

Visual BASIC contains built-in functions to perform many mathematical operations. They allow calculations using such common functions as logarithms, square roots, sines of angles, and so on. As with earlier versions of BASIC, mathematical functions have a three-letter call name followed by a parenthesised argument. They are pre-defined and may be used anywhere in a program. Some of the most common standard functions are listed below.

_____Standard Basic Functions_____

Name	Function
Abs(X)	Returns the absolute value of X
Atn(X)	Arc-tangent of X (1.570796 to −1.570796)
Cos(X)	Cosine of angle X, where X is in radians
Exp(X)	Raises e to the power of X
Int(X)	Returns the truncated integer part of X
Fix()	Returns the integer part of X
Log(X)	Returns the natural logarithm of X
Sgn(X)	Returns 1, 0 or −1 to reflect the sign of X
Sqr(X)	Returns the square root of X
Sin(X)	Sine of angle X, where X is in radians
Tan(X)	Tangent of angle X, where X is in radians
Rnd	Generates a pseudo-random number from 0 to 1, but which does not include 1.

Function calls can be used as expressions or elements of expressions wherever expressions are legal. The argument X of the function can be a constant, a variable, an expression or another function. A more detailed explanation of the use of these functions is given below.

Atn(X):

The arc-tangent function returns a value in radians, in the range +1.570796 to −1.570796 corresponding to the value of a tangent supplied as the argument X. Conversion from radians to degrees is achieved with the relationship Degrees = Radians*180/Pi, where Pi=3.141592654.

Sin(X), Cos(X) and Tan(X):
The sine, cosine and tangent functions require an argument angle expressed in radians. If the angle is stated in degrees, then use the relationship Radians = Degrees*Pi/180.

Sqr(X):
The **Sqr** function returns the square root of the number X supplied to it.

To illustrate the use of some of the above functions, consider a simple problem involving a 2m-long ladder resting against a wall with the angle between ladder and ground being 60 degrees. With the help of simple trigonometry we can work out the vertical distance between the top of the ladder and the ground, the horizontal distance between the foot of the ladder and the wall and also the ratio of the vertical to horizontal distance.

The program uses the trigonometric functions **Sin**, **Cos**, and **Tan**, to solve the problem.

```
Sub Form_Click ()              'Program EXMPLE33.MAK
                               'Ladder against a wall
Dim AngleDeg, AngleRad, Vert, Horiz, Ratio
Pi = 3.141592654

AngleDeg = 60 'in degrees
AngleRad = AngleDeg * Pi / 180   ' In radians
Vert = 2 * Sin(AngleRad)
Horiz = 2 * Cos(AngleRad)
Ratio = Tan(AngleRad)

Print "Original angle = "; AngleDeg; Chr(176)
Print "Vert. distance = "; Format(Vert, "Fixed"); "m"
Print "Hor. distance = "; Format(Horiz, "Fixed"); "m"
Print "Ratio of Vert:Hor. = ";
Print Format(Ratio, "Fixed"); ":1"

End Sub
```

When the program is run and the opened window is clicked, Visual BASIC will respond with

```
Original angle =  60°
Vert. distance =  1.73m
Hor. distance = 1.00m
Ratio of Vert:Hor. = 1.73:1
```

Abs(X):
The **Abs** function returns the absolute (that is, positive) value of a given number. For example **Abs**(1.234) is 1.234, while **Abs**(−2.345) is returned as 2.345.

The **Abs** function can be used to detect whether the values of two variables say, X and Y, are within an acceptable limit by using the statement in the form

```
If Abs(X-Y) < 0.0001 Then
```

in which case the block of statements following the **Then** will be executed only if the absolute difference of the two variables is less than the specified limit, indicating that they are approximately equal. We need to use the **Abs** function in the above statement otherwise a negative difference, no matter how small, would be less than the specified small positive number.

Exp(X):
The exponential function raises the number e to the power of X. The **Exp** function is the inverse of the **Log** function. The relationship is

```
Log(Exp(X)) = X
```

Log(X):
The logarithm to base e is given by the above function. Logarithms to the base e may easily be converted to any other base using the identity

$$\log_a(N) = \textbf{Log}(N)/\textbf{Log}(a)$$

where **log**$_a$(N) stands for the desired logarithm to base a, while **Log**(N) and **Log**(a) stand for the logarithm to the base e of N and a, respectively.

Antilogarithm functions are not provided but they can easily be derived using the following identities:

```
Antilog(X) = e^X    '(base e; this is Exp(X))
Antilog(X) = 10^X   '(base 10)
```

Int(X) and Fix(X):

The integer functions returns the value of X rounded down to the nearest integer. Thus, **Int**(6.97) returns the value 6. The difference between **Int** and **Fix** is that if X is negative, **Int** returns the first negative integer less than or equal to X, but **Fix** returns the first negative integer greater than or equal to X. For example:

```
Int(-5.3) = -6
Fix(-5.3) = -5
```

Fix(X) is equivalent to:

```
Sgn(X) * Int(Abs(X))
```

Numbers can be rounded to the nearest whole number, rather than rounding down, by using the function **Int(**X+0.5**)**. For example, **Int(**5.67+0.5**)** returns the value 6. It can also be used to round to any given number of decimal places, or to the nearest integer power of 10, by using the expression:

```
Int(X*10^D+0.5)/10^D
```

where D is (a) a positive integer or (b) a negative integer supplied by the user. For rounding to the first decimal, D=1; to the nearest 100, D=–2. The program below should help to illustrate these points.

```
Sub Form_Click ()                'Program EXMPLE34.MAK
                                 'Rounding numbers
Dim X  As Double, N As Double
Dim D As Integer
Do
    X = Val(InputBox("Enter any number "))
```

```
          If X = 0 Then End
          D = Val(InputBox("Round to how many places?"))
          N = Int(X * 10 ^ D + .5) / 10 ^ D
          Print N
    Loop Until False
    End Sub
```

Try it yourself. To stop the program enter 0 (zero) in the first Input box, or press its **Cancel** button.

Sgn(X):
The sign function returns 1 if X is positive, 0 if X=0, and −1 if X is negative.

Rnd and Randomize n:
The **Rnd** function is used to produce a pseudo randomly selected number from 0 to 1, but not including 1. The **Randomize** function allows the random-number generator **Rnd** to start from a 'seed number' and produce a series of numbers based on the seed. By using the same seed again, the same series of numbers can be obtained. The statement **Randomize**, by itself, uses the computer's internal clock to seed the random-number generator, while **Randomize n** seeds the random number generator **Rnd** with the number that **n** represents.

Random numbers are used in statistical programs and in all kinds of simulations from simple games to complex computer models. In some programs, especially business simulations, it is necessary to reproduce the same 'random' conditions from run to run. This is done with the 'dice throwing' program given below. Enter the program.

```
Sub Form_Click ()              ' Program EXMPLE35.MAK
                               ' Throwing dice

    Dim I As Integer
    Randomize 2
    Print "THROW",   "NUMBER"
    For I = 1 To 6
        Print I, Rnd
    Next I
End Sub
```

107

Every time it is run, the program produces the same random throws as shown below.

```
THROW          NUMBER
1              1.414126E-02
2              .6076428
3              .3568624
4              .9575312
5              .2980418
6              .7864588
```

In some contexts it is a severe disadvantage to have the same series of random numbers produced. To do this you use the statement

```
Randomize
```

at the beginning of a program. With no seed number given, this function uses the system clock to get its seed, and could be said to be 'truly random'.

In the previous 'dice throwing simulation' the numbers were obviously not integers (as with dice). To produce random integers in a given range, use the formula:

```
Int((Upper - Lower + 1) * Rnd + Lower)
```

where, Upper is the highest number in the range, and Lower is the lowest - for a dice these would be 6 and 1.

Derived Mathematical Functions

Some useful mathematical functions which can be derived from standard Basic functions are listed below:

_____**Derived Mathematical Functions**_____

Function   **Formula**

TRIGONOMETRIC
Cosecant $Csc(X)=1/Sin(X)$
Cotangent $Cot(X)=1/Tan(X)$
Secant $Sec(X)=1/Cos(X)$

INVERSE TRIGONOMETRIC
Arc Cosecant $Acsc(X)=Atn(1/Sqr(X*X-1))+(Sgn(X)-1)*Pi/2$
Arc Cotangent $Acot(X)=-Atn(X)+Pi/2$
Arc Secant $Asec(X)=Atn(Sqr(X*X-1))+(Sgn(X)-1)*Pi/2$

HYPERBOLIC
Hyp Cosine $Cosh(X)=(Exp(X)+Exp(-X))/2$
Hyp Sine $Sinh(X)=(Exp(X)-Exp(-X))/2$
Hyp Tangent $Tanh(X)=-Exp(-X)/(Exp(X)+Exp(-X))*2+1$
Hyp Cosecant $Csch(X)=2/(Exp(X)-Exp(-X))$
Hyp Cotangent $Coth(X)=Exp(-X)/(Exp(X)-Exp(-X))*2+1$
Hyp Secant $Sech(X)=2/(Exp(X)+Exp(-X))$

INVERSE HYPERBOLIC
Arc Cosh $Acosh(X)=Log(X+Sqr(X*X-1))$
Arc Sinh $Asinh(X)=Log(X+Sqr(X*X+1))$
Arc Tanh $Atanh(X)=Log((1+X)/(1-X))/2$
Arc Cosech $Acsch(X)=Log((Sgn(X)*Sqr(X*X+1)+1)/X)$
Arc Cotanh $Acoth(X)=Log((X+1)/(X-1))/2$
Arc Sech $Asech(X)=Log((Sqr(-X*X+1)+1)/X)$

Note: The constant Pi in the above formulae has the value of 3.141592654.

User-Defined Function Procedures:

In some programs it may be necessary to use the same mathematical expression in several places, and often using different data. User-defined functions enable definition of unique operations or expressions. These can then be called in the same manner as standard functions.

A user-defined function is defined as shown in the following example.

```
Function Area (R) As Double
    ' Calculates area of circle of radius R units
    Pi = 3.141592654
    Area = Pi * R ^ 2
End Function
```

Entering it into your program is made very easy; simply typing anywhere on a form, the word **Function**, followed by its Name, will create a new code entry window for the function in the **(general)** section of the form, as shown here.

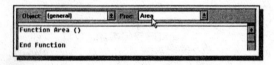

Enter the function and the rest of this small program as shown in the screen dump below.

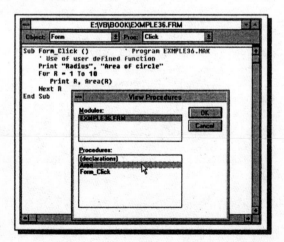

The program calculates the areas of circles with radii of integer values between 1 and 10. The formula is given in the Function Area() statement and the Function is called the same way as Visual BASIC's built-in functions. The value for the radius is passed to the function via a parenthesised variable which in fact could be any legal expression; its value is simply substituted for the function variable.

The bottom example on the facing page also shows the **View Procedures** box opened by pressing **F2** when in Design mode. This gives an easy way to track down the procedures and functions in your program.

Sub Procedures

Visual BASIC supports two kinds of procedures; user-defined functions and Sub-procedures, or Subs. The difference between the two is that a Function returns a value, whereas a Sub is complete in itself. Most of the Visual BASIC code we have seen in this book so far has been made up of Event Procedures, or blocks of program code which are carried out when a certain action is implemented. You can also write your own Subs, which can then be called from anywhere in your program.

You enter a Sub into your program in the same way as described on the previous page for entering Functions (but you type Sub instead of Function).

To illustrate how we can use a Sub-procedure, we will develop a small program which asks for the dimensions of three cylinders and calculates their volumes.

```
Sub Form_Click ()      ' Program EXMPLE37.MAK
                       ' Volume of 3 cylinders
Dim Radius As Double, Height As Double, I As Integer
For I = 1 To 3
    Radius = Val(InputBox("Enter cylinder radius"))
    Height = Val(InputBox("Enter cylinder height"))
    Volume Radius, Height
Next I
End Sub
```

In the above, the Volume statement is calling the following Sub and passing to it the values of Radius and Height.

111

```
Sub Volume (Rad As Double, Ht As Double)
    Dim BaseArea As Double , Vol As Double
    Pi = 3.141592654
    BaseArea = Pi * Rad ^ 2
    Vol = BaseArea * Ht

Print "Cylinder radius = " & Rad & " units"
Print "Cylinder height = " & Ht & " units"
Print "Cylinder volume = " & Vol & " cubic units"
Print
End Sub
```

Note that the Sub above accepted the two arguments, even though they had different names. In older versions of BASIC the Sub would be called with the statement

```
Call Volume (Radius, Height)
```

This is acceptable to Visual BASIC, but the arguments must be enclosed in brackets, as shown. Just remember, no **Call**, no brackets!

After a Sub has been executed, program control is returned to the statement following the calling statement. It is, therefore, possible to build up a library of standard procedures, which can then be invoked from a main program to solve large and complex problems.

Parameter Passing

There are two fundamental rules relating to parameter passing. These are: (a) the number of arguments in an argument list of the calling statement must be the same as that of the formal parameters, and (b) the data type of each argument must match the data type of the corresponding formal parameter.

The formal parameters in a procedure, whether a subprogram or function, are variable names local to that particular procedure. The actual parameter passed to the procedure can either be (i) a variable name local to the calling program or (ii) a literal, constant, or expression.

In the first case, when a parameter is a variable, parameter passing is by 'reference', which means that the address of the variable is passed to the procedure. As the formal parameter within the procedure is also assigned to the same address, this means that any changes to the formal parameter within the procedure can be passed back to the main program.

In the second case, when a parameter is a literal, constant, or an expression, parameter passing is by 'value', which means that the actual value is passed rather than the address in which the value is held. In this case, the value of an expression is calculated, the result is stored in a temporary location and the address of the temporary location is passed to the procedure. As a result, any changes to this parameter by the procedure is only reflected in the temporary address and the original value accessed by the main program remains unmodified.

Subroutines
Subroutines are similar to Sub procedures in many ways but they are not as powerful. They are supported by Visual BASIC primarily because they are the only way that standard BASIC can code frequently used sections of logic into subprograms. Thus, programs written for standard BASIC can be easily adapted to run under Visual BASIC.

The GOSUB and RETURN Statements:
When Basic encounters the **Gosub** statement in the main body of the program, it branches to the first statement of the subroutine, and continues to execute the statements within the subroutine until the **Return** statement is encountered. This diverts program flow to the statement immediately following the **Gosub** statement which called the subroutine. Thus, the **Gosub** statement broadly corresponds to the **Sub** calling statement, while the **Return** corresponds to the **End Sub**.

When successive **Gosub** statements branch to the same subroutine, each time the **Return** statement is reached, the main program is resumed at the last **Gosub** statement from which it branched.

10. WORKING WITH FILES

Programs and 'data files' can be stored on disc quite easily and Visual BASIC allows you to access them from your program front end with the standard Windows file handling dialogue boxes. Before describing this, though, we will spend some time getting to grips with some of the code that needs to be placed behind these file handling dialogue boxes and menus.

Three types of data files can be used to store information, namely sequential, random access or binary files. Each type has advantages and disadvantages. Sequential files use disc space efficiently, but are difficult to update and best used for files which store only text. Random files are less efficient as far as usage of disc space is concerned, but provide quick access to information. Binary files offer great flexibility, but have no structure and, therefore, are difficult to program. We shall investigate the first two of these, by first looking at their individual structure and then by showing how data can be written to, and read from, each type of file.

Sequential Data Files

A sequential data file can be thought of as a one dimensional array with each array location being one byte, capable of holding one character of a string. For example, the name of a friend together with his telephone number

```
ADAMS M. 02-1893
```

could be stored as shown below:

```
Byte                          1                   2
         0 1 2 3 4 5 6 7 8 9 0 1 2 3 4 5 6 7 8 9 0 1
Char     " A D A M S   M . " , " 0 2 - 1 8 9 3 " ¶ ⇓
```

Of special importance to sequential data files are the three ASCII control characters, 10 (linefeed – LF), 13 (carriage return – CR), together shown by the symbol ¶, and 26 (End-of-File marker – EOF), shown above as ⇓. The combination CR/LF (¶) is issued every time you press the <Enter> key.

115

Two friends' names would be stored with details of the second following the first, separated by LF/CR, with the EOF character marking the end of the file. For example,

```
"ADAMS M.","02-1893"¶"SIMS I.","01-1351"¶⇩
```

Carriage returns/linefeeds (¶) mark the end of blocks of information called 'records' with each record containing related information such as names and telephone numbers separated by commas, called 'fields'. Fields can hold any of the different types of variables, such as strings (which appear in quotation marks), integers, long integers, single- and/or double-precision variables.

To write data into a sequential data file you must write a small Visual BASIC program which will 'create' such a file and then 'print' into it the characters representing the information you want to store on disc.

To demonstrate this, we will develop the most simple ASCII text editor imaginable, which treats all the text in the file as one variable.

Open a new project and build the simple form shown below, which has one large Text box and four command buttons.

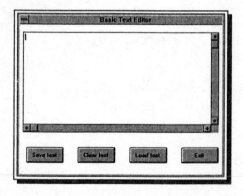

Make sure the *Multiline* property of the Text box is set to True, so that any long lines of text you enter will wrap onto subsequent lines, and then enter the following code.

```
Dim Filename As String    ' General declaration

Sub cmdSave_Click ()       ' Program EXMPLE38.MAK
    ' Save entered file to disc
    Filename = InputBox$("Enter file name")
    Open Filename For Output As #1
    Print #1, Text1.Text
    Close #1
End Sub

Sub cmdLoad_Click ()
    ' Load a text file from disc
    Filename = InputBox$("Enter file name")
    Open Filename For Input As #1
    Text1.Text = Input$(LOF(1), 1)
    Close #1
End Sub

Sub cmdClear_Click ()     ' Clear the text box
    Text1.Text = ""
    Text1.SetFocus
End Sub

Sub cmdExit_Click ()      ' Exit the program
    End
End Sub
```

To test out the program, run it, type a few lines of text into the editing section of the opened window and then save the text by clicking the **Save** button. To check that this worked, you could **Clear** the window and **Load** your file back again, or open your file into the Notebook. Even the Cut and Paste functions work (with their keyboard short-cuts), you can get a lot for a small amount of code with Visual BASIC.

Saving a File to Disc:
In the cmdSave_Click Sub, following the InputBox line, the commands **Open** Filename **For Output As #**1, **Print #**1 and **Close #**1 are all directed to the filing system. The first opens the named file for output, through the communications channel #1. By opening a file, the name of that file is automatically written to the directory of the logged drive. If the filename already exists, the **Open** command will delete its

contents, which means that you lose all the information already stored in that file. Once the data has been written to the file, with the **Print #** command, the file is **Close**d.

Note the special way of writing Visual BASIC commands which are directed to the filing system. They all end with the hash character (#), followed by the channel number n (with values between 1 and 255) through which you communicate with the file. Finally, when you finish with a file you close the communications channel with the **Close #**n command.

Loading a File from Disc:

Once your text file has been created, you must be in a position to read it back into the computer so that your information can be retrieved. This is done, in our example, with the short cmdLoad_Click procedure.

The third line **Open**s the file whose name is held in string variable Filename, for **Input** through channel #1. The next line reads the contents of the whole file using the **Input$** statement. The **LOF(1)** part of the statement gives the length of file to be input. Finally, the file is **Close**d as before.

Common Dialogue Custom Control

As it stands, our text editor is usable but the file handling procedures, by Windows' standards, leave a lot to be desired. With one addition, however, and a few extra lines we can improve it enormously.

The Common Dialogue control shown here (located at the bottom of the Toolbox) allows you to automatically use five of Windows main dialogue boxes in your programs. These are the Open, Save As, Print, Color and Font boxes. We will make use of the first two to improve our editor. In Design mode, drag a Common Dialogue control onto the form of the last example. It doesn't matter where you place it, as, like the Timer, it is invisible at run time. Then edit the code of the Save and Load procedures to that shown on the facing page.

NOTE - Where one line of code will not fit on the book page, the characters '..' have been placed at the end of the book line. Do not type these in, but join the next book line(s) to form one long line in the code entry window.

```
Sub cmdLoad_Click ()    ' Using OPEN dialogue box
    Dim Filename As String
    CMDialog1.Filter = "All Files (*.*)|*.*|Text ..
    Files (*.txt)|*.txt|Batch files (*.bat)|*.bat"
    CMDialog1.FilterIndex = 2
    CMDialog1.Action = 1
    Filename = CMDialog1.Filename
    F = FreeFile
    Open Filename For Input As #F
    Text1.Text = Input$(LOF(F), F)
    Close #F
End Sub

Sub cmdSave_Click ()    ' Using SAVE AS dialogue box
    Dim Filename As String
    CMDialog1.Filter = "All Files (*.*)|*.*|Text ..
    Files (*.txt)|*.txt|Batch files (*.bat)|*.bat"
    CMDialog1.FilterIndex = 2
    CMDialog1.Action = 2
    Filename = CMDialog1.Filename
    F = FreeFile
    Open Filename For Output As #F
    Print #F, Text1.Text
    Close #F
End Sub
```

The first extra line, in both cases, sets the *Filter* property to control what type of files will be displayed in the dialogue boxes. Each filter to be displayed needs a description and the actual filter, separated by the pipe character (|). Make sure you type these two lines above as one long one!

The line

```
CMDialog1.Action = n
```

determines which Windows dialogue box is used, n being selected from the following list.

Setting (n)	*Dialogue Box Displayed*
0	No action
1	Open

2	Save As
3	Color
4	Font
5	Print (needs code to make print)
6	Starts the Windows Help engine.

The dialogue box returns the name of the file selected and stores it in the variable 'Filename' in the line

```
Filename = CMDialog1.Filename
```

The screen dump below shows our program, named EXMPLE39.MAK, using the Save As dialogue box.

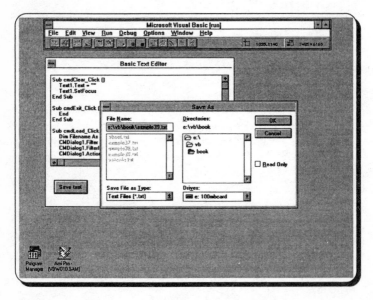

You have probably noticed the use of the line

```
F = FreeFile
```

in our modified code. As Visual BASIC can access up to 255 file channels, it is safer and better practice, to use the **FreeFile** function to return the next file number available for use. If this is passed to a variable (F in our case), the variable can be used whenever a channel # is required.

Random Access Files

Random-access data files are like a collection of equal-length sequential files, which means that each file can have a number of records (each with a record length specified by parameter **Len**). A visual representation of random access data files is shown below:

```
            1         2         3         4
12345678901234567890123456789012345678901234
--------------------------------------------
ADAMS M.                02-1893   iisssssddddddddd
SMITH A. D.             03-864243 iisssssddddddddd
LONGFELLOW A. B. C.  01-5513567iisssssddddddddd
--------------------------------------------
```

In this example, each row represents a record and each record is divided into 5 'fields'. The first field, which is 20 characters long, contains names, the second, which is 10 characters long, contains phone numbers, the third to the fifth field contains numerical data which is encoded to strings of lengths 2, 4 and 8 characters, representing integer, single- and double-precision floating-point numbers, respectively. Thus the record length of each row in the above representation is 44 characters (20+10+2+4+8 = 44).

Defining Records by Type

When using random access, Visual BASIC requires you to define your records with the **Type**..**End Type** declaration. This allows the creation and storage of data in a composite format; mixing string and numeric types. A suitable **Type** definition for the above data would be:

```
Type Record
    Aname As String * 20
    Phone As String * 10
    Units As Integer
    Price As Single
    Amount As Double
End Type
```

121

To open a file and specify its length, with this data would require the following statement:

```
Open Filename For Random As #1 Len = 44
```

As random access is the default for the **Open** statement, the words **For Random** are not strictly required, but we recommend that you get used to including them.

The following program, EXMPLE40.MAK, shows how data sets can be entered into a form and added to a random access file from the form. It is intended more as a demonstration than to perform a really useful task, but the principles can be adapted to almost any kind of consistent format data entry.

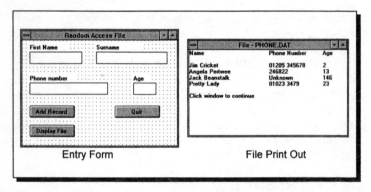

Entry Form   File Print Out

The main form layout is shown above on the left. It consists of four Text boxes to receive the data, each with a Label to identify it, and three Command buttons to control the entry or retrieval of data to and from a file.

Build this form, as shown, and open one more form and a module. These are best opened by clicking the two leftmost buttons on the Toolbar. The second form is used purely to receive printed output from the data file, as shown on the right above.

The module file, with the extension .BAS, is needed to hold the Type definition. Name all the files so that they do not overwrite others in the same directory, and enter the code shown on the next few pages.

This first code is placed in the separate module. It defines a custom data type 'Record'. The **Option Explicit** statement forces Visual BASIC to accept only declared variables.

```
Option Explicit
Type Record
    FirstName As String * 20
    SurName  As String * 15
    Phone As String * 12
    Age As Integer
End Type
```

The next code is for Form1, the 6 **Dim** statements being placed in the general declarations section of the form.

```
Dim Person As Record
Dim RecordLen As Long
Dim F As Integer    ' Filenumber
Dim Msg As String
Dim FileName As String
Dim Position As Integer ' To track record number

Sub Form_Load ()
    ChDrive App.Path
    ChDir App.Path
    RecordLen = Len(Person)
    Msg = "Give file name for data"
    FileName = InputBox$(Msg)
    F = FreeFile
    Open FileName For Random As F Len = RecordLen
    Position = 1
End Sub

Sub cmdAddRecord_Click ()
    GetRecord              ' Load data from text boxes
    Put #F, Position, Person    'Save to file
    Position = Position + 1     'Increase pointer
    txtCName.Text = ""    ' Empty text boxes
    txtSName.Text = ""
    txtPhone.Text = ""
    txtAge.Text = ""
    txtCName.SetFocus
End Sub
```

```
Sub cmdDisplayFile_Click ()
    Dim I As Integer, Caption As String
    Caption = "File - " + UCase$(FileName)
    Form2.Caption = Caption            ' Name window
    Form2.Show            ' Open a print window
    Form2.Print "Name"; Tab(30); "Phone Number";
    Form2.Print Tab(50); "Age"
    Form2.Print
    For I = 1 To Position - 1
        Get #F, I, Person    ' Read a record from file
        ' Trim blanks from and print the record
        Form2.Print Trim$(Person.FirstName);
        Form2.Print " " + Trim$(Person.SurName);
        Form2.Print Tab(30); Trim$(Person.Phone);
        Form2.Print  Tab(50); Trim(Person.Age)
    Next I
    Form2.Print
    Form2.Print "Click window to continue"
End Sub

Sub cmdQuit_Click ()
    Close #F        ' Close the file
    Kill FileName ' Delete file from disc
    End
End Sub

Sub GetRecord ()
    ' Load PERSON variable from text boxes
    Person.FirstName = txtCName.Text
    Person.SurName = txtSName.Text
    Person.Phone = txtPhone.Text
    Person.Age = Val(txtAge.Text)
End Sub
```

The last code, below, is placed in the Click procedure of
Form2. This lets you remove the print window when you are
happy that your data file is working.

```
Sub Form_Click ()
    Form1.txtCName.SetFocus
    Unload Me
End Sub
```

The random access method only works if, after declaring a data Type, you then declare a variable of that type, as done in the line

```
Dim Person As Record
```

The Form_Load Sub is actioned when Form1 is opened at run time. The **ChDrive** and **ChDir** statements set the current drive and directory to that of the application (almost certainly \VB). This is necessary so that the location of the file created is controlled. The line

```
RecordLen = Len(Person)
```

passes the length of our defined data Type to a variable, which is then used in the **Open** statement.

You are then expected to enter data manually into the text boxes. When happy with your data, click the **Add Record** button which actions the cmdAddRecord Sub.

This, first calls the Sub 'GetRecord' which loads the data elements from the text boxes to the respective components of the 'Person' variable. It then **Puts** this data, as one record, into the previously opened file

```
Put #F, Position, Person
```

F represents the channel number used to communicate with the opened file. The 'Position' variable keeps track of the record number being processed, and is incremented after the **Put** operation. The text boxes are then emptied and the focus returned to the first one, so that you can continue to add as many records as you want.

When you want to view all the records entered, click the **Display File** button which activates the cmdDisplayFile Sub. This sets the caption of Form2 and opens it with the **Show** command. The **Get** statement is used to retrieve the data from the file, one record at a time.

```
Get #F, I, Person
```

It is the complement of the **Put** statement. Each record is then **Trim**med, to remove any padding spaces, and printed to the opened Form2 window.

When you have worked out how it all functions, you can press the **Quit** button, which **Closes** the open file and deletes it from your disc with the **Kill** statement. In a working application you would not need this line, but we have added it to save your hard disc getting cluttered.

We have tried to make the code of these examples as simple as possible, to make them easier to understand, so there is no attempt at error trapping or other sophistications.

If you want to develop the programs further, we suggest you first study the two sample programs TEXTEDIT.MAK and RECEDIT.MAK, provided with Visual BASIC.

Binary Files

A binary file is the most rudimentary type of file which offers the greatest flexibility, but its use imposes considerable responsibility on the programmer as binary files do not have any structure. They are a sequence of characters without any delimiters, or records. The characters simply occupy positions 0, 1, 2, and so on, within the file. They are used when you need to keep the size of your data files to the absolute minimum.

Due to their complexity we will not give any more detail on binary files here, as they are a little outside the scope of this book.

11. DEBUGGING YOUR PROGRAMS

As you develop more and more complicated code in your programs you will inevitably make mistakes and produce error messages. There are three types of errors you may encounter as you develop your applications.

Compile Errors:

These occur when your code is incorrectly constructed, such as a **Next** statement without a corresponding **For** statement, or a misspelled word, or a data type mismatch with your variables. Compile errors include syntax errors, which are errors in grammar or punctuation recognised by Visual BASIC and are flagged by the compiler as you attempt to enter the code.

Run-time Errors:

These occur when you attempt to run your program. Common examples include attempting to write to a file that doesn't exist, or dividing by zero.

Logical Errors:

Often the most difficult type of error to correct is when the program doesn't perform as you expect, and produces incorrect results, because your programming logic is at fault.

The first of these error types are sorted out with the help of the compiler when you enter your code into the editor. Run-time and logic errors though, need the help of Visual BASIC's debugging tools, which let you look at the state of the program and all the variables, etc., in the middle of a run.

Break Mode

So far we have encountered two of Visual BASIC's operating modes. Design, when you enter controls and code, and Run when you start it running. There is a third one, Break mode, which is used for most of the debugging processes. You can easily see what mode you are currently in, as it is displayed on the title bar in brackets, as shown on the following page.

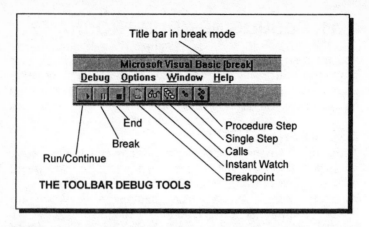

Title bar in break mode

Microsoft Visual Basic [break]

Debug   Options   Window   Help

End
Break
Run/Continue

Procedure Step
Single Step
Calls
Instant Watch
Breakpoint

THE TOOLBAR DEBUG TOOLS

At any time a program is running you can change to Break mode by clicking the Break icon on the Toolbar. While in Break mode you can edit and debug your code and usually continue execution of the program. If not you have to restart the program.

The Debug Tools
The best way to get a rapid overview of the debugging possibilities of Visual BASIC is to spend ten minutes with the program tutorial. To do this, use the **Help**, **Learning Microsoft Visual Basic** menu command and click the **Debugging Your Application** menu button.

Work your way through the presented screens which have been very professionally put together and show several working examples of debugging in practice.

Breakpoints:
You can set breakpoints in your code in Design mode to halt your program execution at those points and check the values of variables or see what actions will be taken next.

To set a breakpoint place the insertion point anywhere in a line of code where you want the program to stop and use the

Debug, **Toggle Breakpoint** command, the **F9** function key, or click the Breakpoint toolbar icon. Visual BASIC adds the breakpoint and highlights the line.

Using the Debug Window:

To execute code in the Debug window **while in break mode** you simply type a line of code in the Debug window and press <Enter> to execute the statement.

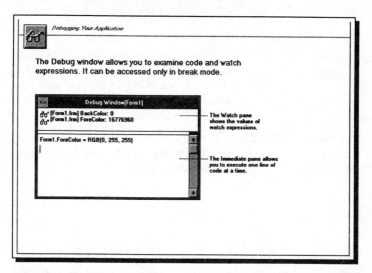

While in the Debug window, you can do most of the things you do in the Code window, but statements in the Debug window are not saved with the project.

Using Instant Watch:

While in break mode, you may want to check the current value of a variable or expression, this is easy to do using the Instant Watch command.

 To display an instant watch, highlight an expression in either the Code window or the Immediate pane of the Debug window (shown above) and click the Instant Watch toolbar icon. A dialogue box should open displaying the current value of the expression.

Calls:

 If you ever get code that includes nested procedures you may be glad of the Calls facility which helps to trace any active procedure calls in your program.

Tracing Execution:

Visual BASIC's tracing tools are very useful as it is not always obvious, with an object oriented program, which statement will be executed next. The following two procedures are best actioned from their Toolbar icons.

Single Step

Steps through each line of code, including procedures, and stops. You can see what code is actioned and, if you have Watches set, you can see the effect of each statement on the program variables.

Procedure Step

Steps through your code as above, but treats each procedure as if it were a single statement.

APPENDIX A
THE VATCALC.MAK CODE

All the code and property details for the two forms of the example program VATCALC.MAK are included here, as created with the **File**, **Save File As** menu command, with the **Save As Text** option selected in the dialogue box. Some extra formatting has been added to make the code easier to follow.

NOTE - Where one line of code will not fit on the book page, the continuation characters '..' have been placed at the end of the book line. Do not type these in, but join the next book line(s) to form one long line in the code entry window.

```
Begin Form frmVatCalc
    BorderStyle     =    1   'Fixed Single
    Caption         =    "VAT Calculator"
    ClientHeight    =    3465
    ClientLeft      =    1860
    ClientTop       =    2085
    ClientWidth     =    4005
    Height          =    4155
    Left            =    1800
    LinkTopic       =    "Form1"
    MaxButton       =    0   'False
    ScaleHeight     =    3465
    ScaleWidth      =    4005
    Top             =    1455
    Width           =    4125

Begin TextBox Text3
    BorderStyle     =    0   'None
    Height          =    285
    Left            =    2760
    TabIndex        =    7
    TabStop         =    0     'False
    Top             =    1080
    Width           =    1215
End
```

```
Begin TextBox Text2
    BorderStyle      =    0    'None
    Height           =    285
    Left             =    2760
    TabIndex         =    8
    TabStop          =    0    'False
    Top              =    720
    Width            =    1215
End

Begin CommandButton Command1
    Caption          =    "&Calculate"
    Default          =    -1   'True
    Height           =    375
    Left             =    1200
    TabIndex         =    2
    Top              =    1560
    Width            =    1215
End

Begin CommandButton Command3
    Caption          =    "C&lear"
    Height           =    375
    Left             =    1200
    TabIndex         =    3
    Top              =    2760
    Width            =    1215
End

Begin CommandButton Command2
    Caption          =    "&Exit"
    Height           =    375
    Left             =    1200
    TabIndex         =    4
    Top              =    2160
    Width            =    1215
End

Begin TextBox Text1
    ForeColor        =    &H000000FF&
    Height           =    285
    Left             =    2160
    TabIndex         =    0
```

```
         Top            =    240
         Width          =    1335
   End

   Begin Label Label1
      Caption         =    "Enter amount"
      Height          =    255
      Left            =    840
      TabIndex        =    1
      Top             =    240
      Width           =    1215
   End

   Begin Label Label3
      Height          =    255
      Left            =    240
      TabIndex        =    6
      Top             =    1080
      Width           =    2415
   End

   Begin Label Label2
      Height          =    255
      Left            =    240
      TabIndex        =    5
      Top             =    720
      Width           =    2295
   End

   Begin Menu mnuOptions
      Caption         =    "&Options"
         Begin Menu mnuVATRate
            Caption         =    "&VAT Rate"
         End
         Begin Menu mnuAbout
            Caption         =    "&About"
         End
         Begin Menu mnuExit
            Caption         =    "E&xit"
         End
   End
End
```

```vb
Dim Cost As Currency ' Dimensions in general section
Dim CostPlus As Currency
Dim Costless As Currency
Dim VATRate As Double
Dim NVATRate As Double

Sub Command1_Click ()
' Check to see if VAT rate has been changed.
    If NVATRate > 0 Then
        VATRate = NVATRate
    Else VATRate = 17.5
    End If
    Cost = Val(Text1.Text)
    CostPlus = Cost * (1 + VATRate / 100)
    Costless = Cost / (1 + VATRate / 100)
    MsgPlus = "Amount plus " & VATRate & "% VAT = "
    MsgLess = "Amount less " & VATRate & "% VAT = "
    Label2.Caption = MsgPlus
    Text2.Text = CostPlus
    Label3.Caption = MsgLess
    Text3.Text = Costless
    Text1.Text = Format$(Cost, "currency")
    Text2.Text = Format$(CostPlus, "currency")
    Text3.Text = Format$(Costless, "currency")
End Sub

Sub Command2_Click ()
    End     ' Leave the VAT calculater
End Sub

Sub Command3_Click ()   'Clear text areas
    Text1.Text = ""
    Text2.Text = ""
    Text3.Text = ""
    Label2.Caption = ""
    Label3.Caption = ""
    Text1.SetFocus
End Sub

Sub mnuAbout_Click ()
' Places text in the About box. All the CaptionText
' variables are concatenated with the Chr$(10) line
' feed characters, to display the text.
```

```
        CaptionText1 = "SIMPLE VAT CALCULATOR"
        CaptionText2 = "PRMO - 1995"
        CaptionText3 = "VAT rate is set at"
        CaptionText4 = "17.5%. Use the menu"
        CaptionText5 = "option to change it."
        frmAbout!lblAbout.Caption = CaptionText1 &..
        Chr$(10) & Chr$(10) & CaptionText2 & Chr$(10) &..
        Chr$(10) & CaptionText3 & Chr$(10) &..
        CaptionText4 & Chr$(10) & CaptionText5
        ' Show (with style = 1) is used to display the
        ' form as modal. Unloading it is handled in the
        ' form's cmdOK_Click event procedure.
        frmAbout.Show 1
End Sub

Sub mnuExit_Click ()
        End     ' Leave the VAT calculater
End Sub


Sub mnuVATRate_Click ()
' Get new VAT rate from user.
NVATRate = Val(InputBox$("Enter new VAT rate"))
VATRate = NVATRate
End Sub


Begin Form frmAbout
        BackColor       =   &H00C0C0C0&
        BorderStyle     =   1   'Fixed Single
        Caption         =   "About"
        ClientHeight    =   3705
        ClientLeft      =   2610
        ClientTop       =   1710
        ClientWidth     =   3855
        ClipControls    =   0       'False
        ControlBox      =   0       'False
        Height          =   4110
        Left            =   2550
        LinkTopic       =   "Form1"
        MaxButton       =   0       'False
        MinButton       =   0       'False
        ScaleHeight     =   3705
```

```
     ScaleMode        =    0   'User
     ScaleWidth       =    3851.005
     Top              =    1365
     Width            =    3975

Begin CommandButton cmdAbout
     Cancel           =    -1   'True
     Caption          =    "OK"
     Default          =    -1   'True
     Height           =    495
     Left             =    1440
     TabIndex         =    1
     Top              =    3000
     Width            =    975
End

Begin Frame fraAbout
     BackColor        =    &H00C0C0C0&
     Height           =    2415
     Left             =    240
     TabIndex         =    0
     Top              =    240
     Width            =    3375

   Begin Label lblAbout
       Alignment      =    2   'Centered
       BackStyle      =    0   'Transparent
       Height         =    2535
       Left           =    120
       TabIndex       =    2
       Top            =    240
       Width          =    3135
       End

   End

End

Sub cmdAbout_Click ()
' This form is loaded as modal. The program will
' not continue until this button is actioned.
' The Unload statement is used here to unload form
' from memory when the user clicks this button.
    Unload frmAbout
End Sub
```

APPENDIX B
THE EVENT PROCEDURES

The following is a complete alphabetic list of the event triggered procedures of Visual BASIC, where an event is an action which is recognised by a form or control. The event name is substituted in the procedure declaration as follows

Sub ControlName_**EventName** (arguments)

Event	*Description*
Activate	Occurs when a form becomes the active window.
Change	Indicates that the contents of a control have changed.
Click	Occurs when the user clicks (presses and then releases) a mouse button over an object.
DblClick	Occurs when the user quickly double clicks a mouse button over an object.
Deactivate	Occurs before a different form becomes the active window.
DragDrop	Occurs when a drag-and-drop operation is completed by dragging a control over a form or other control.
DragOver	Occurs when a drag-and-drop operation is in progress. Can be used to monitor when the mouse pointer enters, leaves, or is directly over a valid target.
DropDown	Occurs when the list portion of a combo box is about to drop down; this event does not occur if a combo box's Style property is set to 1 (Simple Combo).

Error	Occurs only as the result of a data access error that occurs when no Visual BASIC code is being executed.
GotFocus	Occurs when an object receives the focus, either by tabbing to or clicking on the object, or with the SetFocus method in code.
KeyDown	Occurs when the user presses a key while an object has the focus. Used with the KeyPress event.
KeyPress	Occurs when the user presses and releases a key, with an ANSI code.
KeyUp	Occurs when the user releases a key while an object has the focus. Used with the KeyPress event.
LinkClose	Occurs when a DDE conversation terminates.
LinkError	Occurs when there is an error during a DDE conversation.
LinkExecute	Occurs when a command string is sent by a destination application in a DDE conversation.
LinkNotify	Occurs when the source has changed the data defined by the DDE link, (destination LinkMode property set to 3 - Notify).
LinkOpen	Occurs when a DDE conversation is being initiated.
Load	Occurs when a form is loaded.
LostFocus	Occurs when an object loses the focus, either by tabbing to or clicking on the object, or in code with the SetFocus method.

MouseDown	Occurs when the user presses a mouse button.
MouseMove	Occurs when the user moves the mouse.
MouseUp	Occurs when the user releases a mouse button.
Paint	Occurs when part, or all, of a form or picturebox is exposed after it has been moved or enlarged, or after a window that was covering the object has been moved.
PathChange	Occurs when the path changes by setting the FileName or Path properties from code.
PatternChange	Occurs when the file filter (e.g. "*.*") has changed by setting the FileName or Pattern properties from code.
QueryUnload	Occurs before a form or application closes.
Reposition	Occurs after a record becomes the current record.
Resize	Occurs when a form first appears or the size of an object changes.
RowColChange	Occurs when the currently active cell changes to a different cell.
Scroll	Occurs while a user drags the box on a scroll bar.
SelChange	Occurs when the selected range changes to a different cell or range of cells.
Timer	Occurs when a preset interval for a timer control has elapsed.
Unload	Occurs when a form is about to be removed from the screen.

Updated	Occurs when an object's data has been modified.
Validate	Occurs before a different record becomes the current record; before the Update method (except when data is saved with the UpdateRecord method); and before a Delete, Unload or Close operation.

APPENDIX C
LANGUAGE REFERENCE

The following is a complete list of Visual BASIC's reserved function, statement and method key-words. Where a **function** is a standard procedure that performs a specific task and returns a value; a **statement** is a reserved word which forms part of a complete expression indicating one kind of action, declaration, or definition; and a **method** is a Visual BASIC reserved word that acts on a particular object.

For more detailed information on any of these key-words we suggest you search the Visual BASIC Help facility. This includes working examples of them all.

Those expressions with '(Pro)' alongside are only available in the Professional Edition of Visual BASIC.

Abs Function
Returns the absolute value of a number.

AddItem Method
Adds a new item to a list or combo box, or adds a new row to a grid control at run time.

AddNew Method
Clears the copy buffer in preparation for creating a new record in a Table or Dynaset.

AppActivate Statement
Activates an application window.

Append Method (Pro)
Adds a new object to a collection.

AppendChunk Method
Appends data from a String to a Memo or Long Binary field in the copy buffer of a specified Table or Dynaset.

Arrange Method
Arranges the windows or icons within an MDI Form.

Asc Function
Returns a numeric value that is the ANSI code for the first character in a string expression.

Atn Function
Returns the arctangent of a number.

Beep Statement
Sounds a tone through the computer's speaker.

BeginTrans Statement
Begins a new transaction.

Call Statement
Transfers program control to a Visual Basic Sub procedure or a dynamic-link library (DLL) procedure.

CCur Function
Explicitly converts expressions to the Currency data type.

CDbl Function
Explicitly converts expressions to the Double data type.

ChDir Statement
Changes the current default directory on a specified drive.

ChDrive Statement
Changes the current drive.

Choose Function
Selects and returns a value from a list of arguments.

CInt Function
Explicitly converts expressions to the Integer data type.

Chr, Chr$ Function
Returns a one-character string whose ANSI code is the argument.

Circle Method
Draws a circle, ellipse, or arc on an object.

Clear Method
Clears the contents of a list or combo box, or clears the contents of the operating environment Clipboard.

Clone Method (Pro)
Returns a duplicate record set object that refers to the same record set from which it was created.

CLng Function
Explicitly converts expressions to the Long data type.

Close Method
Closes a specified Database, QueryDef, or record set.

Cls Method
Clears graphics and text generated at run time from a form or picture.

Command, Command$ Function
Returns the argument portion of the command line used to launch Microsoft Visual BASIC.

CommitTrans Statement
Transcends the current transaction.

CompactDatabase Statement
Compacts and encrypts or decrypts a Microsoft Access database.

Const Statement
Declares symbolic constants for use in place of values.

Cos Function
Returns the cosine of an angle (angle in radians).

CreateDatabase Function (Pro)
Creates a Microsoft Access database, and returns a Database object that is open for exclusive read/write access.

CreateDynaset Method (Pro)
Creates a Dynaset object from a specified Table object, QueryDef object, or SQL statement.

CreateQueryDef Method (Pro)
Creates a new QueryDef in a specified database.

CreateSnapshot Method (Pro)
Creates a Snapshot object from a specified table, QueryDef, or SQL statement.

CSng Function
Explicitly converts expressions to the Single data type.

CStr Function
Explicitly converts expressions to the String data type.

CurDir, CurDir$ Function
Returns the current path for the specified drive.

CVar Function
Explicitly converts expressions to the Variant data type.

CVDate Function
Converts an expression to a Variant of VarType 7 (Date).

Date, Date$ Functions
Returns the current system date.

Date, Date$ Statement
Sets the current system date.

DateAdd Function
Returns a Variant containing a date to which a specified time interval has been added.

DateDiff Function
Returns a Variant containing the number of time intervals between two specified dates.

DatePart Function
Returns a specified part of a given date.

DateSerial Function
Returns the date serial for a specific year, month, and day.

DateValue Function
Returns the date represented by a String argument.

Day Method
Returns an integer between 1 and 31, inclusive, that represents the day of the month for a date argument.

DDB Function
Returns the depreciation of an asset for a specific period using the double-declining balance method.

Declare Statement
Declares references to external procedures in a dynamic-link library (DLL).

DefInt Statement
Sets the default data type as Integer.

DefLng Statement
Sets the default data type as Long.

DefSng Statement
Sets the default data type as Single.

DefDbl Statement
Sets the default data type as Double.

DefStr Statement
Sets the default data type as String.

DefVar Statement
Sets the default data type as Variant.

Delete Method
Deletes the current record in a specified Table or Dynaset.

DeleteQueryDef Method (Pro)
Deletes a specified QueryDef from a database.

Dim Statement
Declares variables and allocates storage space.

Dir, Dir$ Function
Returns the name of a file or directory that matches a specified pattern and file attribute.

Do...Loop Statement
Repeats a block of statements while a condition is true or until a condition becomes true.

DoEvents Function, **DoEvents** Statement
Causes Visual Basic to yield execution so that Windows can process events.

Drag Method
Begins, ends, or cancels dragging controls.

Edit Method
Opens the current record in a specified record set for editing by copying it to the copy buffer.

End Statement
Ends a Visual Basic procedure or block.

EndDoc Method
Terminates a document sent to the Printer, releasing it to the print device or spooler.

Environ, Environ$ Function
Returns the string associated with an operating system environment variable.

EOF Function
Returns a value during file input that indicates whether the end of a file has been reached.

Erase Statement
Reinitialises the elements of fixed arrays and deallocates dynamic-array storage space.

Err, Erl Function
Returns error status.

Err Statement
Sets Err to a specific value.

Execute Method
Invokes an action query in a specified database.

ExecuteSQL Method
Executes an action query SQL statement in a specified database.

Exit Statement
Exits a Do...Loop, a For...Next loop, a Function procedure, or a Sub procedure.

Exp Function
Returns e (the base of natural logarithms) raised to a power.

FieldSize Method
Returns the number of bytes in a text or binary field.

FileAttr Function
Returns file mode or operating system file information about an open file.

FileCopy Statement
Copies a file.

FileDateTime Function

Returns a String that indicates the date and time a specified file was created or last modified.

FileLen Function

Returns a Long integer that indicates the length of a file in bytes.

FindFirst Method

Locates the first record that satisfies specified criteria and makes that record the current one.

FindLast Method

Locates the last record that satisfies specified criteria and makes that record the current one.

FindNext Method

Locates the next record that satisfies specified criteria and makes that record the current one.

FindPrevious Method

Locates the previous record that satisfies specified criteria and makes that record the current one.

Fix Function

Returns the integer portion of a number.

For...Next Statement

Repeats a group of instructions a specified number of times.

Format, Format$ Function

Formats a number, date, time, or string according to instructions contained in a format expression.

FreeFile Function

Returns the next valid unused file number.

FreeLocks Statement

Suspends data processing, allowing a database to release locks on record pages and make all data in the local Dynaset objects current in a multi-user environment.

Function Statement

Declares the name, arguments, and code that form the body of a Function procedure.

FV Function

Returns the future value of an annuity based on periodic, constant payments and a constant interest rate.

Get Statement

Reads from a disc file into a variable.

GetAttr Function

Returns an integer that indicates a file, directory, or volume label's attributes.

GetChunk Method

Returns all or a portion of a Memo or Long Binary field in a specified record set.

GetData Method

Returns a picture from the Clipboard object.

GetFormat Method

Returns an integer indicating whether there is an item in the Clipboard matching a specified format.

GetText Method

Returns a text string from the Clipboard.

Global Statement

Used in the Declarations section of a module to declare global variables and allocate storage space.

GoSub...Return Statement

Branch to, and return from, a subroutine within a procedure.

GoTo Statement

Branches to a specified line within a procedure.

Hex, Hex$ Function

Returns a string that represents the hexadecimal value of a decimal argument.

Hide Method

Hides a form, but does not unload it.

Hour Function

Returns an integer between 0 and 23, inclusive, that represents the hour of the day corresponding to the time provided as an argument.

If...Then...Else Statement
Allows conditional execution, based on the evaluation of an expression.

IIf Function
Returns one of two parts depending on the evaluation of an expression.

Input, Input$ Function
Reads characters from a sequential file.

Input # Statement
Reads data from a sequential file and assigns it to variables.

InputBox, InputBox$ Function
Displays a prompt in a dialogue box and returns input from the user.

InStr Function
Returns the position of the first occurrence of one string within another string.

Int Function
Returns the integer portion of a number.

IPmt Function
Returns the interest payment for a given period of an annuity based on periodic, constant payments and a constant interest rate.

IRR Function
Returns the internal rate of return for a series of periodic cash flows.

IsDate Function
Returns a value indicating whether or not a Variant argument can be converted to a date.

IsEmpty Function
Returns a value indicating whether or not a Variant variable has been initialised.

IsNull Function
Returns a value that indicates whether or not a Variant contains the special Null value.

IsNumeric Function
Returns a value indicating whether or not a Variant variable can be converted to a numeric data type.

Kill Statement
Deletes file(s) from a disc.

LBound Function
Returns the smallest available subscript for the indicated dimension of an array.

LCase, LCase$ Function
Returns a string in which all letters of an argument have been converted to lowercase.

Left, Left$ Function
Returns the leftmost n characters of a string argument.

Len Function
Returns the number of characters in a string expression or the number of bytes required to store a variable.

Let Statement
Assigns the value of an expression to a variable.

Line Input # Statement
Reads a line from a sequential file into a String or Variant variable.

Line Method
Draws lines and rectangles on an object.

LinkExecute Method
Sends a command string to the other application in a dynamic data exchange (DDE) conversation.

LinkPoke Method
Transfers the contents of a control to the source application in a dynamic data exchange (DDE) conversation.

LinkRequest Method
Asks the source in a dynamic data exchange (DDE) conversation to update the contents of a control.

LinkSend Method
Transfers the contents of a picture control to the destination application in a dynamic data exchange (DDE) conversation.

ListFields Method (Pro)
Creates a Snapshot with one record for each field in a specified record set.

ListIndexes Method (Pro)
Creates a Snapshot with one record for each field in each index in a specified table.

ListParameters Method (Pro)
Creates a Snapshot with one record for each parameter in a specified QueryDef object.

ListTables Method (Pro)
Creates a Snapshot with one record for each Table or QueryDef in a specified database.

Load Statement
Loads a form or control into memory.

LoadPicture Function
Loads a picture into a form, picture box, or image control.

Loc Function
Returns the current position within an open file.

Lock, Unlock Statement
Controls access by other processes to an opened file.

LOF Function
Returns the size of an open file in bytes.

Log Function
Returns the natural logarithm of a number.

LSet Statement
Left aligns a string within the space of a string variable, or copies a variable of one user-defined type to another variable of a different user-defined type.

LTrim, LTrim$ Function
Returns a copy of a string with leading spaces removed.

Mid, Mid$ Function

Returns a string that is part of some other string.

Mid, Mid$ Statement

Replaces part of a string with another string.

Minute Function

Returns an integer between 0 and 59, inclusive, that represents the minute of the hour corresponding to the time provided as an argument.

MIRR Function

Returns the modified internal rate of return for a series of periodic cash flows.

MkDir Statement

Creates a new directory.

Month Function

Returns an integer between 1 and 12, inclusive, that represents the month of the year for a date argument.

Move Method

Moves a form or control.

MoveFirst, MoveLast, MoveNext, MovePrevious Method

Moves to the first, last, next, or previous record in a specified record set and makes that record current.

MsgBox Function

Displays a message in a dialogue box, waits for the user to choose a button and returns a value indicating which button was pressed.

MsgBox Statement

Displays a message in a dialogue box and waits for the user to choose a button.

Name Statement

Changes the name of a disc file or directory.

NewPage Method

Ends the current page and advances to the next.

Now Function

Returns a date that represents the current date and time according to the computer's system clock.

NPer Function
Returns the number of periods for an annuity based on periodic, constant payments and a constant interest rate.

NPV Function
Returns the net present value of an investment based on a series of periodic cash flows and a discount rate.

Oct, Oct$ Function
Returns text that represents the octal value of the decimal argument.

On Error Statement
Enables an error-handling routine and specifies the location of the routine within a procedure.

On...GoSub, On...GoTo Statement
Branches to one of several specified lines, depending on the value of an expression.

Open Statement
Enables input/output (I/O) to a file.

OpenDatabase Function (Pro)
Opens an existing database and returns a Database object.

OpenQueryDef Method (Pro)
Opens a specified QueryDef for editing.

OpenTable Method (Pro)
Opens an existing table and returns a Table object.

Option Base Statement
Declares the default lower bound for array subscripts.

Option Compare Statement
Declares the default comparison mode to use when string data is compared.

Option Explicit Statement
Forces explicit declaration of all variables.

Partition Function
Returns a string indicating where a number occurs within a calculated series of ranges.

Pmt Function
Returns the payment for an annuity based on periodic, constant payments and a constant interest rate.

Point Method
Returns the RGB colour of the specified point on a form or picture box.

PopupMenu Method
Displays a pop-up menu on a form at the current mouse location, or at specified coordinates.

PPmt Function
Returns the principal payment for a given period of an annuity based on periodic, constant payments and a constant interest rate.

Print # Statement
Writes data to a sequential file.

Print Method
Prints a text string on an object using the current colour and font.

PrintForm Method
Sends a bit-for-bit image of a non-MDI form to the printer.

PSet Method
Sets a point on an object to a specified colour.

Put Statement
Writes from a variable to a disc file.

PV Function
Returns the present value of an annuity based on periodic, constant payments to be paid in the future and a constant interest rate.

QBColor Function
Returns the RGB colour code corresponding to a colour number.

Randomize Statement
Initialises the random-number generator.

Rate Function
Returns the interest rate per period for an annuity.

ReDim Statement

Used at the procedure level to declare dynamic-array variables and allocate or reallocate storage space.

Refresh Method

Forces an immediate update of a form, control, or object.

RegisterDatabase Statement

Makes connect information for an ODBC data source name available for use by the OpenDatabase function.

Rem Statement

Used to include explanatory remarks in a program.

RemoveItem Method

Removes an item from a list or combo box, or removes a row from a grid control, at run time.

RepairDatabase Statement

Attempts to repair a corrupted Microsoft Access database.

Reset Statement

Closes all disc files.

Resume Statement

Resumes program execution after an error-handling routine is finished.

RGB Function

Returns a long integer representing an RGB colour value.

Right, Right$ Function

Returns the rightmost n characters of a string argument.

RmDir Statement

Removes an existing directory.

Rnd Function

Returns a random number, between 0 and 1.

Rollback Method

Ends the current transaction and restores the database to the state it was in when the transaction began.

RSet Statement

Right aligns a string within the space of a string variable.

RTrim, RTrim$ Function
Returns a copy of a string with trailing (rightmost) spaces removed.

SavePicture Statement
Saves a picture from a form, picture box, or image control into a file.

Scale Method
Defines the co-ordinate system for an object.

Second Function
Returns an integer between 0 and 59, inclusive, that represents the second of the minute for a time argument.

Seek Function
Returns the current file position.

Seek Statement
Sets the position in a file for the next read or write operation.

Select Case Statement
Executes one of several statement blocks depending on the value of an expression.

SendKeys Statement
Sends one or more keystrokes to the active window as if they had been entered at the keyboard.

Set Statement
Assigns an object reference to a variable.

SetAttr Statement
Sets attribute information for a file.

SetData Method
Puts a picture in the Clipboard using the specified format.

SetDataAccessOption Statement
Sets a global option for data access usage.

SetDefaultWorkspace Statement
Establishes the user ID and password for protected (security-enabled) Microsoft Access databases.

SetFocus Method
Sets the focus to a form or control.

SetText Method
Puts a text string in the Clipboard using the specified Clipboard format.

Sgn Function
Returns an integer indicating the sign of a number.

Shell Function
Runs an executable program.

Show Method
Displays a form.

Sin Function
Returns the sine of an angle (angle in radians).

SLN Function
Returns the straight-line depreciation of an asset for a single period.

Space, Space$ Function
Returns a string consisting of a specified number of spaces.

Spc Function
Skips a specified number of spaces in a Print # statement or Print method.

Sqr Function
Returns the square root of a number.

Static Statement
Used at the procedure level to declare variables and allocate storage space. Variables declared with the Static statement retain their value as long as the program is running.

Stop Statement
Suspends execution of the running Visual BASIC code.

Str, Str$ Function
Returns a string representation of the value of a numeric expression.

StrComp Function
Returns a Variant indicating the result of the comparison of two string arguments.

String, String$ Function
Returns a string whose characters all have a given ANSI code or are all the first character of a string expression.

Sub Statement
Declares the name, arguments, and code that form the body of a Sub procedure.

Switch Function
Evaluates a list of expressions and returns a value or an expression associated with the first expression in the list that is True.

SYD Function
Returns the sum-of-years' digits depreciation of an asset for a specified period.

Tab Function
Used with the Print # statement and the Print method to advance the print position.

Tan Function
Returns the tangent of an angle (angle in radians).

TextHeight Method
Returns the height of a text string as it would be printed in the current font of an object.

TextWidth Method
Returns the width of a text string as it would be printed in the current font of an object.

Time, Time$ Function
Returns the current system time.

Time, Time$ Statement
Sets the system time.

Timer Function
Returns the number of seconds that have elapsed since 12:00 a.m. (midnight).

TimeSerial Function
Returns the time serial for a specific hour, minute, and second.

TimeValue Function
Returns the time represented by a String argument.

Trim, Trim$ Function
Returns a copy of a string with both leading and trailing spaces removed.

Type Statement
Defines a user-defined data type containing one or more elements.

UBound Function
Returns the largest available subscript for the indicated dimension of an array.

UCase, UCase$ Function
Returns a string with all letters of an argument converted to uppercase.

Unload Statement
Unloads a form or control from memory.

Update Method
Saves the contents of the copy buffer to a specified Table or Dynaset.

UpdateControls Method
Gets the current record from a data control's record set and displays the appropriate data in controls bound to a data control.

UpdateRecord Method
Saves the current values of bound controls.

Val Function
Returns the numeric value of a string of characters.

VarType Function
Returns a value that indicates how a Variant is stored internally by Visual BASIC.

Weekday Function

Returns an integer between 1 (Sunday) and 7 (Saturday) that represents the day of the week for a date argument.

While...Wend Statement

Executes a series of statements in a loop as long as a given condition is true.

Width # Statement

Assigns an output-line width to a file.

Write# Statement

Writes data to a sequential file.

Year Function

Returns an integer between 100 and 9999, inclusive, that represents the year of a date argument.

ZOrder Method

Places a specified form or control at the front or back of the z-order within its graphical level.

INDEX

164

NOTES

NOTES

NOTES

NOTES

COMPANION DISCS TO BOOKS

COMPANION DISCS are available for most books written by the same author(s) and published by BERNARD BABANI (publishing) LTD, as listed at the front of this book (except for those marked with an asterisk). These books contain many pages of file/program listings. There is no reason why you should spend hours typing them into your computer, unless you wish to do so, or need the practice.

COMPANION DISCS come in 3½" format with all example listings.

ORDERING INSTRUCTIONS

To obtain your copy of a companion disc, fill in the order form below or a copy of it, enclose a cheque (payable to **P.R.M. Oliver**) or a postal order, and send it to the address below. Make sure you fill in your name and address and specify the book number and title in your order.

Book No.	Book Name	Unit Price	Total Price
BP		£3.50	
BP		£3.50	
BP		£3.50	
Name		Sub-total	£.............
Address:		P & P (@ 45p/disc)	£.............
		Total Due	£.............
Send to: P.R.M. Oliver, CSM, Pool, Redruth, Cornwall, TR15 3SE			

PLEASE NOTE

The author(s) are fully responsible for providing this Companion Disc service. The publishers of this book accept no responsibility for the supply, quality, or magnetic contents of the disc, or in respect of any damage, or injury that might be suffered or caused by its use.